T0318477

Cambridge Elements ☰

Elements in the Problems of God
edited by
Michael L. Peterson
Asbury Theological Seminary

GOD, SALVATION, AND THE PROBLEM OF SPACETIME

Emily Qureshi-Hurst
University of Oxford

CAMBRIDGE
UNIVERSITY PRESS

Shaftesbury Road, Cambridge CB2 8EA, United Kingdom

One Liberty Plaza, 20th Floor, New York, NY 10006, USA

477 Williamstown Road, Port Melbourne, VIC 3207, Australia

314–321, 3rd Floor, Plot 3, Splendor Forum, Jasola District Centre, New Delhi – 110025, India

103 Penang Road, #05–06/07, Visioncrest Commercial, Singapore 238467

Cambridge University Press is part of Cambridge University Press & Assessment, a department of the University of Cambridge.

We share the University's mission to contribute to society through the pursuit of education, learning and research at the highest international levels of excellence.

www.cambridge.org
Information on this title: www.cambridge.org/9781009269582

DOI: 10.1017/9781009269612

First published 2022

A catalogue record for this publication is available from the British Library.

ISBN 978-1-009-26958-2 Paperback
ISSN 2754-8724 (online)
ISSN 2754-8716 (print)

Cambridge University Press & Assessment has no responsibility for the persistence or accuracy of URLs for external or third-party internet websites referred to in this publication and does not guarantee that any content on such websites is, or will remain, accurate or appropriate.

God, Salvation, and the Problem of Spacetime

Elements in the Problems of God

DOI: 10.1017/9781009269612
First published online: October 2022

Emily Qureshi-Hurst
University of Oxford

Author for correspondence: Emily Qureshi-Hurst,
emily.qureshi-hurst@pmb.ox.ac.uk

Abstract: Much has been written on the relationship between the nature of temporal reality and the God of Classical Theism. Despite the popularity of this general area, what the physics and metaphysics of spacetime might mean for specific theological doctrines has received less attention. Recently, however, interest in this rich and dynamic interplay of ideas has seen rapid growth. This Element provides both an introduction to the physics and metaphysics of spacetime and a jumping-off point for understanding how these can – and in fact should – inform both Christian theology and the philosophy of religion more generally. The author will argue that the nature of spacetime raises particular and pressing problems for Christianity, specifically the interrelated doctrines of salvation and eschatology, and explore whether adequate solutions to these problems are available.

This Element also has a video abstract: www.cambridge.org/qureshi-hurst

Keywords: time, spacetime, salvation, eschatology, science and religion

ISBNs: 9781009269582 (PB), 9781009269612 (OC)
ISSNs: 2754-8724 (online), 2754-8716 (print)

Contents

Introduction

Time is an incontrovertibly central feature of our lived experience, and yet the concept itself is notoriously hard to define. We structure our daily lives using clock time. We plan for our long-term futures with the expectation that those abstract futures will become present, concrete, realities. We contextualise our life's events within narratives formed from our past experiences, although these experiences have vanished into the irretrievable past. Time, then, is of fundamental importance to our conceptualisation both of our identities and of the world we inhabit. Yet when asked 'what is time?' many might struggle to give more than a superficial definition. This is reflected in the intellectual study of time, and its remarkable failure to provide many conclusive answers to even the most basic temporal questions.

It has been noted by several scholars that the philosophy of time is rather unusual in that most of its core problems have not been conclusively resolved. Why is this so? One reason might be that there are several competing ways one could go about answering questions about the nature of time. One might take a metaphysical approach by attempting to articulate, using logic and rational arguments, exactly of what temporal reality consists. One might take a linguistic approach, assessing our use of temporal language and what this might reveal about the underlying temporal structures that language seeks to describe. One might take a psychological approach using introspection on our temporal phenomenology, or, more recently, psychological experiments on time perception. Or, one could take a scientific approach, using observational data and mathematical formalism to form a physical theory of time. The problem is, each of these approaches yields different, sometimes incompatible, results.

In the distant past, philosophers disagreed completely about what metaphysics revealed about time. Some argued that the universe is constantly in flux (and therefore time passes) whilst others claimed that reality (including time) is static and unchanging. Many modern thinkers are in similar disagreement. Our temporal experience seems to indicate that time does pass, whereas some of our most successful empirical theories say the opposite. One's endorsement of a temporal theory may well depend upon whether one believes experience or physics should cast the deciding vote between rival explanations. Perhaps the issue is that we are fundamentally limited by our inability to step outside of the bounds of time and examine it from an external, objective, perspective.

Whilst this problem is not going away, trying to find answers to these ancient and open questions is still a valuable pursuit, especially for the theist. For one, the universe is fundamentally temporal. Therefore, most important theological questions are at least tangentially related to the nature of time, as these issues concern the relation between creature and creator. For example: is God within time, experiencing it as it unfolds? Or is God outside of time, viewing all moments at once? In the former, God is immanent but subject to time's passage. In the latter, God is sovereign but distanced from creation. One's understanding of the nature of time will inform how one goes about answering these theological questions.

Philosophy, however, is no longer the only method by which one can approach temporal reality. The natural sciences are now expertly equipped with both observational data and highly fine-tuned equations that allow a far more precise probing of time than had previously been possible. Indeed physics, specifically Einstein's special and general theories of relativity, indicate that time is one dimension of the more fundamental spacetime. The most widely accepted ontology of spacetime is that all spacetime points (all spatial and temporal locations) tenselessly exist, with none having a more metaphysically privileged status than any other. In other words, a so-called B-theory or block universe view of reality is correct. On this view, time does not really pass.

The nature and structure of spacetime are deeply relevant to how specific doctrines should be understood, though this is a far less well-studied area than 'God and time' more generally. Consider the Christian notion of personal salvation, namely the type of salvific process that happens (or at least begins to happen) in an individuals' spatio-temporal lifetime. Such a process requires an objective change or transformation from fallen to saved. If time does really pass, then the Christian doctrine of personal salvation is relatively unproblematic. An individual can change from being fallen to being saved throughout the course of their life, and this change is substantiated by the objective temporal passage that renders 'fallenness' *past* and 'salvation' *present*. Yet if time does not pass, and change is not objective, then a personal salvific transformation from fallen to saved is problematised. One can no longer say which of the incompatible properties one possesses – individuals are both fallen *and* saved because both states exist *simpliciter* and neither state can claim objective priority (at least from a temporal perspective).

The doctrine of eschatology also faces problems. If time does not pass, and all moments of time tenselessly exist, then the entirety of the spatio-temporal universe always exists and can be redeemed eschatologically by God as Christian doctrine describes. No problem there, then. If time *does* pass, however, *and* the past vanishes into obscurity, then physical theories predicting that the universe will end either in heat death (freeze) or a big crunch (fry) raise serious questions about the plausibility of eschatology traditionally understood. Neither 'freeze' nor 'fry' can accommodate bodily resurrection or the eschatological transformation of physical reality into a 'new creation'

(2 Corinthians 5:17) as people, objects, and events will have disappeared into the non-existent past and been rendered irretrievable by the destruction or degradation of the universe.

Therefore, the metaphysics of time and the physics of spacetime are highly relevant to certain core components of both Christian theology and the philosophy of religion. In this Element I will sketch out some of leading arguments in the philosophy and physics of time, particularly those that relate to spacetime. Although these are foreshadowed in classical temporal metaphysics, modern physics brings these problems into sharp relief. I will explore these issues from the perspective of the interdisciplinary field of Science and Religion, giving particular consideration to the challenges raised for the nature of God and the coherence of the interrelated Christian doctrines of salvation and eschatology.

This Element is both an introduction to the physics and metaphysics of time and a jumping-off point for understanding how these can – and in fact should – inform both Christian theology and the philosophy of religion more generally. I will argue that the nature of spacetime raises particular and pressing problems for Christianity, such as those briefly alluded to above. In order to engage in a dialogue of this kind, I believe that science and theology must be translated into a common language. That language is philosophy. As Paul Tillich astutely remarked: 'the point of contact between scientific research and theology lies in the philosophical element of both' (Tillich 1951: 21). The method and content of this Element, then, will be largely philosophical.

Taking seriously a realist interpretation of spacetime and the physical theories that support it raises highly significant questions about the nature of God, the nature and scope of human salvation, and the possibility of eschatological redemption for all physical creation. Thus, spacetime offers a rich and dynamic resource for understanding the Christian doctrines of salvation and eschatology in the context of contemporary physics and the problems that arise therein. Whether the theist can respond is yet another of the philosophical study of time's open questions; one which I hope the reader will be better equipped to answer after reading this Element. In order to understand the rich and dynamic relationship between God, salvation, and spacetime, we must begin by laying the metaphysical groundwork. To that task we now turn.

1 The Metaphysics of Time

It makes sense to begin with metaphysical reflections on the nature of time for three reasons. First, these discussions pre-date physical approaches to examining time, and so beginning here makes chronological sense. Second, temporal metaphysics provides conceptual apparatus that will help situate the physics of time in the broader contexts that are of concern in this work. Third, up until the twentieth century, philosophical reflections on time were frequently intertwined with theology. Thus, the history of temporal metaphysics is highly relevant to any exploration of the relationship between God, salvation, and spacetime.

1.1 Time in Ancient Philosophy

Metaphysical reflections on time's nature can be traced back to the pre-Socratic philosophers Heraclitus and Parmenides, each of whom was writing around the fifth century BCE. Parmenides was committed to a static temporal ontology of *being*, whilst Heraclitus advocated a dynamic ontology of *becoming*. Though neither developed a fully fledged theory of time by contemporary standards, their radically conflicting ideas about central metaphysical issues are, in many ways, mirrored in temporal metaphysics today.

Heraclitus maintained a proto-empiricist commitment to the reliability of sensory experience in relaying facts about the external world. We perceive everything as constantly changing with the passage of time, and this experience should be trusted (even though our ordinary language and logic are largely unable to adequately describe it). Thus, Heraclitus developed a doctrine of flux whereby impermanence is universal. Everything is in a constant state of transition – we can never encounter the same object or person twice, for all things are always changing. In short, the only constant is change itself.

As we only have disjointed excerpts of his work, a certain amount of reconstruction of his views has been necessary. Indeed, Heraclitus' most famous soundbite, 'one cannot step twice in the same river', is documented not in a primary source but in Plutarch's *On The 'E' at Delphi* (392b) and Plato's *Cratylus* (402a). The fragmented form through which we receive his writings means that one cannot be certain of Heraclitus' views. It is, however, generally accepted that he was committed to a dynamic ontology that emphasised the ubiquity of impermanence (Hoy 2013).

Heraclitus' contemporary Parmenides, who is generally understood to be the father of metaphysics, held the opposing view that reality is ultimately singular, unified, and unchanging. His metaphysical writings also survive only in fragments. Nevertheless, what we do have indicates that Parmenides was a monist who believed reality was comprised of a single, unchanging, substance. In rejecting change as no more than an illusion, he stood in opposition to Heraclitus.

Parmenides argued that change requires the passage of time because an entity possessing different properties at different times necessitates some objective change between those times. If we claim that some entity will change in the future, then we claim that the future is real and can generate new entities or new properties of existing entities (as something cannot come from nothing). Yet we contradict ourselves by elsewhere thinking of the future and past as non-real – if something is real, we think of it as real now, if something is in the future then it is not yet real and if it is in the past then it is no longer real. So, to think of the past and future is to think of what is *not*. Otherwise, nothing would distinguish the future from the present. Parmenides concludes, therefore, that nothing can come into or go out of existence, nor can entities objectively change, without committing simultaneously to both the existence and non-existence of the future. But the future cannot both exist and not exist. Therefore, talking temporally leads to contradiction, and time and change cannot be mind-independently real features of reality.

Further arguments to this end were developed by Parmenides' student Zeno who devised a series of famous paradoxes commonly known as 'Zeno's Paradoxes'. These paradoxes of motion, received primarily through Aristotle's writing on them, were devised to unearth a fundamental inconsistency in our common understanding of both motion and change. Consider the paradox of The Dichotomy, which involves an athlete running a race. In order to finish, the runner must first cover half the distance between the starting point and the finish line; however, to reach the halfway point she must travel halfway between her starting point and the halfway point. This process of dividing the race into segments that must be traversed can be repeated *ad infinitum*, leading to the conclusion that the runner must cover an infinite number of finite distances in a finite amount of time. This insurmountable task means she could never complete the race. But, of course, people never encounter such problems in the real world, and therein lies the paradox. Parmenides and Zeno conclude from this (and other similar paradoxes) that although it *appears* to us that the world contains motion and change, reason and logic rule out the possibility of either being mind-independent features of reality (Bardon 2013: 10–12; Strobach 2013).

Aristotle, whose writings on the nature of reality shaped the Western intellectual landscape for many centuries, rejected Zeno's paradoxes and their denial of change (and thus also of time). To understand his argument, we must first set out how he characterised time. Aristotle's definition of time is typically translated as the 'number of motion according to before and after' (Aristotle *Physics* 219b 1–2). The Greek word *kinesis*, however, encompasses more than just motion, referring also to qualitative changes such as a change in colour (Strobach 2013: 30). According to Aristotle, then, time is the numerical measurement of motion and/or change. He also argued that without change of any kind, we would not be aware of the passage of time. From this we can infer that Aristotle understood time as relational – we use time to count, order, and measure durations of and changes between events, but time is not independent of these. If everything in the universe vanished or stood still, time too would cease.

Aristotle's refutation of Zeno's paradoxes claims that they rest on a conflation between time itself (an abstract numerical measure) and the things it measures (concrete change and motion). If time is a unit of measurement, then it is a mathematical quantity that does not necessarily correspond perfectly with material objects. The Dichotomy, Aristotle argued, confuses the infinite divisibility of numerical values (i.e. that there are an infinite number of values between the integers 1 and 2) with the idea that physical objects such as racetracks are comprised of an infinite number of smaller and smaller physical parts. Similarly, with units of time, whilst one can infinitely divide the numbers used to measure temporal duration, this does not mean that any given duration is actually composed of an infinite number of finite units of time. Zeno's paradoxes fail to distinguish between the abstract numerical system one uses as a temporal measure and the concrete reality, namely change, that is being measured in units of time. Thus, Aristotle maintained the existence of change, and the inextricable connection between it and time (Bardon 2013: 12–17).

Aristotle and Heraclitus' commitment to a dynamic conception of reality can be read as seminal forms of contemporary theories of time that assert temporal passage as fundamental. The Parmenides-type view is echoed in current theories of time that deny temporal passage, re-imagine our common-sense understanding of change, and do away with an objective distinction between tenses. This latter position claims that all moments of time eternally coexist in a so-called block universe. It is worth noting that there are important differences between these ancient disagreements about the nature of temporality and debates happening between modern theories of time. Nevertheless, these embryonic explorations of whether reality changes or not were important first steps in the philosophical quest to understand the nature of reality and the temporal dimension by which it is structured.

1.2 Time in Medieval Philosophy

The philosophy of the medieval period (or Middle Ages) was characterised by a deep religiosity, and most notable contributors to the study of time were writing from an explicitly theistic standpoint. It is in the writing of these scholars that contemplating the relationship between God and time, and time and theology more generally, really began. In this section I will sketch out the views of four leading contributors to medieval discourse on the nature of time: St Augustine of Hippo, Anicius Manlius Severinus Boethius, Anselm of Canterbury, and St Thomas Aquinas.

St Augustine of Hippo (354 CE–430 CE) was a Christian philosopher writing during the transition period between late antiquity and the medieval era. Whilst Augustine technically falls just outside the boundaries of the medieval period, his thought was so influential in shaping medieval theology that he can be appropriately placed in this section. We find Augustine's thoughts on the nature of time in the autobiographical *Confessions* in which he engaged philosophically with his conversion to Christianity. He introduces the topic of time by noting that it is elusive and hard to define: 'what, then, is time? If no one asks me, I know: if I wish to explain it to one that asks, I know not' (Augustine 2005). Importantly, Augustine distinguishes between divine eternity and created temporality – the former is true time experienced by God, whilst the latter is an imperfect but necessary consequence of our creaturely predicament.

The temporal content of *Confessions* cannot be neatly placed under a single temporal theory of the kind that dominates contemporary analytic philosophy (see Section 1.3). Perhaps this is due to the self-professed difficulty with which Augustine grappled with time. In various places he uses language consistent with a dynamic temporal ontology and in other places he seems to claim that such dynamism is only a perceptual quality of the mind. We remember the past and anticipate the future, directly experiencing only the present. It is in the mind, specifically in the cognitive states of memory, attention, and anticipation, that we measure time's passing and conceive of a difference between the tenses.

Augustine seems to have believed that such dynamic experience, fragmented as it is into past, present, and future, is a consequence of our creaturely limitations. God created the universe, including time, out of nothing, and is not subject to change as temporal beings are. For the perfect and immutable God, there is no distinction between tenses; nothing passes, and all moments are held together in a timeless present. Divine time is eternal (atemporal, durationless, unified) and stands over and above, and is ontologically superior to, created time. Whilst our senses 'flutter between the motions of things past and things still to come', God dwells in 'the glory of everfixed eternity' – these states are radically different in kind and cannot be compared (Augustine 2005).

It is precisely this idea that divine time is not mind-independently dynamic or tensed that has led some scholars to place Augustine's thought within the class of static theories of time (Helm 2014: 147–54). Augustine believed that the omniscient God saw reality as it truly is. If God does not experience time dynamically, and our creaturely experience of temporality is subjective, then one may infer that Augustine understood mind-independent time as static and unchanging. On this view, all moments of created time exist *simpliciter* and with equal ontological status. God has perfect knowledge of all moments of time because all moments of time exist tenselessly in front of him (so to speak).

He knows them simply by observing them. Nevertheless, Augustine's views on time are complex and multifaceted, and he does not unambiguously fit into the static or dynamic camp. What can be said with certainty, however, is that he believed in a fundamental ontological distinction between created time and divine eternity, and that the former is (at least mind-dependently) tensed and dynamic whilst the latter is neither.

Anicius Manlius Severinus Boethius (c.475–7 CE–c.526 CE), more commonly known simply as Boethius, was also a key figure in the transition between late antiquity and the Latin medieval period who had a seismic influence on medieval thought. His masterpiece, *Consolations of Philosophy*, was written whilst he was in prison, under sentence of death, on the false charges of treason and performing magic. Born into a wealthy family, Boethius was well-educated in matters of Greek philosophy, and his work contains unmistakable Platonic and Stoic influences. Unlike Augustine, who wrestled with the impenetrability of both time and eternity, Boethius viewed time, eternity, and their relationship, as relatively straightforward and unproblematic.

Boethius defined eternity as 'the complete possession all at once of illimitable life', going on to say that 'this becomes clearer by comparison with temporal things. For whatever lives in time proceeds as something present from the past into the future, and there is nothing placed in time that can embrace the whole extent of its life equally' (Boethius *Consolation:* Book V, Prose 6). From this definition Eleonore Stump draws out four components: (1) anything eternal has a life, (2) the life of an eternal being cannot be limited by beginning or end, (3) eternity involves infinite duration, (4) an eternal being possesses all its life at once, meaning it cannot be temporal (Stump 2003: 133–4).

This definition, which formed the foundation of all subsequent medieval reflections on eternity, was developed whilst thinking through the problem of divine foreknowledge. God is omnipotent and so knows all things, including future events. Yet if God knows what I will do before I do it, then it seems as though I am not really freely making a choice (as I could have done nothing else). As freedom is integral to moral and soteriological responsibility, this is a significant concern. Boethius solved this problem by arguing that God has perfect knowledge of the future because he is outside of time and views all events tenselessly. He compared God's apprehension of all temporal events to the vision one might have of a landscape atop a mountain.

According to some interpreters, Boethius' view is notably distinct from the view that because God is outside time, he experiences no kind of temporality at all. God's mental life is neither bounded by creaturely temporality nor completely divorced from time altogether. Whilst we experience the present as a tiny fleeting instant, God holds all moments of time together at once in the eternal divine present of beginningless, endless, infinity. This defines two modes of existence – creaturely existence which is temporal (viz. dynamic, tensed, ordered by relations of *before* and *after*), and divine existence which is eternal (viz. possessing all life at once in the eternal present). Some have understood the eternal present as atemporal *simpliciter*, namely a durationless instant, whilst others have argued that it is a (seemingly contradictory) atemporal present of infinite duration. In the 1980s, Eleonore Stump and Norman Kretzmann defended and developed this latter interpretation in conversation with Einstein's theory of relativity with intriguing, though not uncontroversial, results (see Section 3.3) (Stump and Kretzmann 1981: 433).

Anselm of Canterbury (1033–1109) also reflected on the relation between divine eternity and creaturely temporality. Along with other medieval thinkers, Anselm was committed to the doctrine of divine simplicity whereby God is a perfect metaphysical unity, his nature is equal to his attributes, and he is not comprised of parts (temporal or otherwise). Rather, God is the uncaused cause – being itself – who set the world into motion with his creative volition. This means that neither his personhood nor his experiential perspective can be split into 'what is', 'what has been', and 'what will be'.

From divine simplicity follows divine immutability. In *Proslogion* Anselm presented his famous definition of God as a being than which no greater can be conceived (which has since been developed into the ontological argument for God's existence). If God is a perfect being, then he cannot change, because any change would necessarily be a form of degeneration. As change is inextricably bound-up with time, a changeless God cannot be temporal. Anselm partook in the medieval consensus that, on the basis of these doctrines, God must be timelessly eternal.

There is an ongoing debate amongst interpreters as to Anselm's views on the structure of created time. Brian Leftow, for example, reads Anselm as a proponent of the doctrine that only the present (and present things) exist – the past and future are unreal. He refers to Anselm's definition of the present as 'fleeting', and his description of that present as passing away into the not-present, to make his case (Leftow 2009: 297–8). Katherin Rogers, however, reads Anselm as arguing that reality is comprised of a four-dimensional 'block' in which all moments of time and points in space tenselessly exist. Anselm writes that God sees all moments in time at once, which Rogers interprets as an ontological commitment to the coexistence of all times. Our temporal experience of a fleeting present is, on her view, a consequence of creaturely limitations and is devoid of ontological content (Rogers 2007: 3). A third reading simply denies that Anselm was in the business of temporal metaphysics at all, arguing that he was actually concerned with purifying the notion of divine eternity from imperfections imposed upon it by creaturely language (Bobier 2021). I encourage the interested reader to wade through this hermeneutical quagmire and decide for themselves Anselm's conception of time.

St Thomas Aquinas (1225–1274) is the medieval philosopher-theologian whose enduring impact on Christian theology is second to none. His writings on time can be delineated into two points of focus: his discussion of divine eternity, and his treatment of the relation between God and temporal creation. He develops his understanding of the former apophatically – God has no beginning or end, God does not experience succession or change, God does not experience temporality as he is always in the eternal now. Along with most other medieval philosophers, Aquinas endorses both Boethius' definition of eternity and the classical theological doctrines of divine simplicity and immutability, leading him to the same conclusions as Anselm. Aquinas' interpretation of Boethian eternity, Eleonore Stump argues, is one of infinite duration, rather than an atemporal, eternal, instant (Stump 2003: 135–6).

Aquinas' views on the relation between God and creation have more positive content. Once again influenced by Boethius, he considers this issue in the context of the problem of divine foreknowledge and human freedom. And, like Boethius, he solves the problem by claiming that all times (past, present, and future) are present to God at once. In this way, God atemporally knows all temporal events, including the free choices of human agents. This can be imagined using the analogy of a circle. As a point at the centre of a circle is related to all points on the circle's circumference, so too can God be said to be simultaneous with, and thus have perfect knowledge of, each point in temporal reality that is laid out before him. Nor does God have to experience succession, a temporal property, in order to experience all moments of dynamic time and know how these are related to each other. He writes:

> God, however, is wholly outside the order of time, stationed as it were at the summit of eternity, which is wholly simultaneous, and to Him the whole course of time is subjected in one simple intuition. For this reason, He sees in one glance everything that is affected in the evolution of time, and each thing as it is in itself, and it is not future to Him in relation to His view as it is in the order of its causes alone (although He also sees the very order of the causes).
> (Aquinas *Commentary, I Peri Hermeneias:* Lesson 14)

For this reason, William Lane Craig has conjectured that Aquinas is a so-called temporal B-theorist, meaning that he believed all moments of time coexist and temporal reality can be reduced to fixed temporal ordering relations between events (see Section 1.3). Craig makes this claim by arguing that God's apprehension of all events at once is not merely an epistemic consequence of divine omniscience. It also has ontological ramifications, namely that God can apprehend all events at once because they all *actually exist* at once. Nevertheless, there are excerpts in which Aquinas seems to endorse something like the dynamic, A-theory of time that maintains the unreality of the future (Craig points out this apparent contradiction in Aquinas' writings).

Leftow offers a more charitable yet rather anachronistic interpretation of Aquinas which uses a concept from special relativity, namely the relativity of simultaneity (see Section 2.1), to deny that Aquinas was either inconsistent or a B-theorist about time (Leftow 1990). On this view, God's 'seeing' of all moments of time is epistemic, with no ontological consequences for the concurrent existence of all those moments. Whichever of these interpretations one endorses, it remains the case that Aquinas sits within a venerable tradition of medieval philosophers who, for theological reasons, hold the following: (1) God is outside of time, (2) divine time is characterised by a Boethian-type eternity, (3) this divine eternity is of a radically different ontological kind to the temporality of creation.

There were many others writing on time, eternity, and creation in the medieval period both within and external to the Christian tradition. For a helpful overview, see (McGinnis 2013). It has been necessary to set out these seminal thinkers' approaches to the nature of time and its relation to Christian theology and the philosophy of religion, as these ideas have reverberated through all subsequent scholarship. With the ancient and medieval groundwork laid, we are now able to jump forward many centuries to survey the contemporary philosophical landscape with an appreciation of its origins.

1.3 Time in Twentieth and Twenty-First-Century Philosophy

There is a great gulf between medieval conceptions of time and how twentieth-century analytic philosophers approach the issue. In jumping from Aquinas to the modern day, several important contributors to the discourse on time's nature have been set aside. This is an unfortunate consequence of space restrictions, and the interested reader should turn to (van Fraassen 1985: 58–104; Brook 2013; Gallagher 2013) to begin to supplement the gaps in this Element.

Most analytic philosophy of time published in the twentieth century has been written in the long shadow cast by a seminal article written by J. M. E. McTaggart in (1908). McTaggart's famous article distinguished between three systems of ordering positions in time: (1) by their possession of the properties *past, present,* and *future.* (2) In accordance with the two-place relations *earlier than, later than,* and *simultaneous with.* (3) In accordance with three-place relations of temporal *betweenness.*

McTaggart called the temporal series that holds (1) to be fundamental to any description of time the A-series. On the A-series time passes, and events possess the properties of being future, then present, then past. He named the temporal series that describes events in time with recourse only to the relations contained in (2) the B-series. The B-series holds that the temporal ordering relations *earlier than, later than,* and *simultaneous with* (viz. B-relations) are the most fundamental constituents of time. On the B-series, describing events in time in accordance with such relations, and not objective tensed properties, is sufficient to account for time's fundamental structure. The system for describing time contained in 3), namely a description via only the relations of temporal betweenness, is known as the C-series. Though it has received significantly less scholarly attention than the A-series and B-series, it is being taken increasingly seriously (Farr 2020). The C-series denies both that time passes and that time is objectively directional. Instead, a complete description of time can be given by accounting for which events are between one another. A rainbow, for example, contains a sequence of colours that makes sense read in either direction; the C-series makes an analogous claim regarding events in time. The distinction between the A-series, B-series, and C-series sits at the heart of contemporary debates in the philosophy of time. Although there are many nuances in temporal metaphysics, it is fair to say that subsequent scholarship has reified these temporal series (along with various metaphysical and linguistic claims) into fully fledged metaphysical theories: the A-theory, B-theory, and C-theory.

Though there are several A-theories, all claim that (1) time is *dynamic* in that it passes or flows, (2) tense is objectively real, and (3) that there is an objective and universal present moment we call *now.* Each specific A-theory is formed by a different combination of metaphysical claims, although all share the Heraclitan commitment to a dynamic temporal ontology and the Aristotelian connection between time and change. Presentism claims that only the present exists; it is the objective frontier of becoming that separates a vanished past with a not-yet-realised future. The Growing Block view accepts the reality of the past but denies the reality of the future. Growing Block theorists claim that *now* is the objective point at which a non-real future emerges, and previous present moments are added to the real 'block' of past events (which is always growing). The Moving Spotlight claims that all temporal points coexist, but that some times are more special than others. As a spotlight moving across a street illuminates each house in turn, so too does flowing time pick out 'nows' which are metaphysically privileged, and this constitutes the passage of time.

There is less variation in the B-theory, which claims that all moments of time coexist in a block universe. It is tenseless, static, and eternalist, meaning it (1) denies the objective reality of tense, (2) rejects that time flows or passes, and (3) claims all moments in time tenselessly exist like points in space. The C-theory is also committed to a block universe metaphysic, but denies that this block universe has any objective temporal order. Rather, it can be 'read' in either direction without losing something fundamentally temporal. Each of these shares Parmenides' commitment to a static temporal ontology.

McTaggart argued that time was unreal, as (1) the A-series is fundamental to time and (2) the A-series is self-contradictory. Nevertheless, most contemporary philosophers do not accept his rather radical conclusion about the unreality of time, instead choosing to reject (1) if they subscribe to the B-theory or C-theory, and reject (2) if they subscribe to the A-theory. The *Cambridge Elements in Metaphysics* volume on *Time* contains an expert in-depth assessment of McTaggart's argument and its lasting legacy (Dyke 2021). I refer the interested reader there to learn more about this truly seminal piece of philosophy.

Another important debate taking place in contemporary philosophy of physics is whether time and space, or more accurately *spacetime*, is an entity that exists independently of the objects and events within it. The substantivalist answer: yes. On this view spacetime is basic, meaning it is an important component of the fundamental entities in the universe and has an ontological status independent of material objects. An early proponent of such a view was Isaac Newton (see Section 2) who defended at length the claim that space and time were receptacles in which objects dwelled, rather than being merely derivable from relations between those objects. The relationalist, on the other hand, understands spacetime to be reducible to the various spatio-temporal relations between material entities. On this view, if no physical objects, entities, or events existed, then spacetime, too, would not exist.

The Leibniz–Clarke correspondence, a series of letters between Samuel Clarke (a Newtonian substantivalist) and Gottfried Wilhelm Leibniz (a relationalist), was an early example of the type of debates still transpiring between these two camps. This epistolary discourse is still considered one of the most important in early modern physics. Today, discourse on relationalism and substantivalism is firmly grounded in the philosophy of physics, particularly of Einstein's general theory of relativity (see Section 2.3).

Interest is also growing in temporal phenomenology, particularly whether our temporal experience is veridical or illusory. The centrality of temporal experience is illustrated by A.N. Prior's famous example of the sharp phenomenological distinction between anxious anticipation of a future event and relief when the event has passed. Prior writes that the relief one feels when thinking 'thank goodness that's over' cannot be explained tenselessly. One is not feeling relief that one's utterance is in an *after than* relation with some dreaded event (say, a painful dental procedure), rather one feels relief that the procedure *is in one's past* and does not have to be experienced anymore. Thus, our experience seems tensed, that is, more consonant with an A-theory of time. Not only is our experience structured by apprehensions of tense, but, as Barry Dainton points out, our phenomenological apprehension of the world possesses a fundamentally dynamic character. We are conscious of a continuity of sounds, sights, and sensations. One moment and its sensory contents flow into the next, creating a so-called stream of consciousness and a corresponding stream of experience (Dainton 2011: 385).

It is not universally agreed upon that we experience time as though it passes, and in recent years, studies have been carried out in order to examine this question in detail (Latham, Miller, and Norton 2019, 2020). However, many philosophers do endorse the claim that we experience temporal passage, of which there are two parts. First, (it seems that) there is an objective present moment, and second, which instant seems present keeps changing – we experience now as moving along a series of times from earlier to later times. Whether this experience has ontological content is a matter of much debate.

A-theorists generally have the least to say about temporal experience, as they claim both that (a) we experience time as passing and (b) this is because time actually passes. So, there is no real problem that requires addressing. Presentist William Lane Craig, for example, has called our temporal experience a properly basic belief. Properly basic beliefs, developed by Alvin Plantinga as part of his Reformed Epistemology, work like mathematical axioms in our epistemic structures. They are foundational, forming the basis of all other knowledge, and do not require evidential or inferential justification to be warranted. Rather, they are typically self-evident or immediately apparent to the senses. In the case of passage phenomenology, Craig argues that our experience is so 'irreducibly present' that all arguments against it fail. Temporal experience is a 'defeater defeater' meaning it overwhelms any defeaters brought against it (Craig 2000: 165). Upon the rational, true belief that time passes, we construct much of the rest of our knowledge.

B-theorists and C-theorists seem to face bigger problems than A-theorists in explaining temporal experience. If time does not pass, then whence passage phenomenology? Answers to this question can be delineated into two camps: (1) illusionism and (2) veridicalism. Illusionism holds that we do experience time as passing, and that this is illusory. Veridicalism denies this. Instead, the veridicalist holds that we experience features of the world like succession, order, and duration, and this is all our temporal experience amounts to. As such, there is no illusion to explain away, and our temporal experience is sufficiently accounted for by tenseless facts.

Adolf Grünbaum, a twentieth-century metaphysician, argued that we do experience time as passing but that this is not evidence for an A-theory of time. He argued that *nowness* depends fundamentally on experience – some event *e* does not become, and cannot be understood as happening *now,* unless a conscious agent experiences *e* (and is aware of experiencing *e* as present) or experiences an event *f* that is simultaneous with *e* (and is aware of experiencing *f* as present). By experiencing successive subjectively defined presents, dynamic temporal experience is generated. As such, he located the source of temporal experience in the mind's subjective interpretation of the world as apprehended through sensory experience, rather than some ontological feature of mind-independent reality. He called nowness 'mind-dependent', showing that he occupied the illusionism camp (Grünbaum 1967: 384).

Subsequent scholarship has built upon Grünbaum's proposal. Robin Le Poidevin, for example, argues that the B-theorist can explain passage phenomenology through a coupling of directly experiencing an event as present and a very recent memory of a prior event. This generates a stream of consciousness that appears to the perceiver like temporal passage (Le Poidevin 2007). Laurie Paul argues similarly that our experience of passage, though central to our subjective perspective, is an illusion generated by visual perception and mental representation of successive, though static, events (Paul 2010: 333). She argues that we should think of temporal experience as akin to the way motion pictures or time-lapse photography generate dynamic films from many still frames. Our temporal experience, on her view, is generated by our brains through experiencing cognitive inputs from a series of static events and tenseless facts. On illusionism, then, we do experience time as though it passes, but our (dynamic) temporal experience can be explained without reference to (dynamic) temporal ontology.

Veridicalism, on the other hand, holds that our temporal experience accurately represents the objective nature of time in some important way. Veridicalists deny both that our experience of time is dynamic and that we experience time as though it is dynamic. Therefore, our experience is veridical; there is no illusion that requires explanation. The source of temporal experience is the succession, order, and duration of events. As succession is an objective property of events on the B-theory, namely events are ordered by the relations *earlier than, later than,* and *simultaneous with,* our experience is veridical. But as those real features of the world are not A-properties or tensed facts, Veridicalism (of this type) remains B-theoretic. Veridicalist Natalja Deng characterises nowness as akin to hereness – there is no illusion in my thinking that I am *here* at my desk typing away, though *here* is not an ontologically privileged location. Similarly, on Veridicalism, I am under no illusion when I also believe myself to be typing *now.* There is no objective now, as there is no objective here, but from my observational perspective, both are real and shape my experience in important ways (Deng 2019b).

The problem of temporal experience is hardest to address for the C-theorist, as they can appeal neither to dynamic time nor tenseless but time-directed B-relations to substantiate our experience of temporal passage. Matt Farr suggests several ways that one can be a C-theorist and account for passage phenomenology, which are:

> '(1) our experience of time constitutes the illusion that time is directed; or (2) our temporal experience coupled with background beliefs give rise to the false belief that time appears to be directed; or (3) it is simply useful to talk as though our experience of things is directed from past to future; or (4) the world appears to us exactly as though the C-theory were true' (Farr forthcoming: 27).

I encourage the interested reader to turn to Farr's chapter on this for further details on the various candidate explanations. Debates between A-theorists, B-theorists, and C-theorists over their various explanations of temporal experience rage on. It is undeniable that the issue of passage phenomenology is a lively area in the philosophy of time at present. See Dyke (2021: chapter 6) to delve deeper into these issues.

The twentieth and twenty-first centuries have seen a significant rise in interest in the philosophy of time. The previous paragraphs have, albeit briefly, set out some of that philosophical landscape, although there are many other notable landmarks besides the ones covered. An excellent introductory resource that can fill in these gaps is (Baron and Miller 2019). Perhaps one of the most significant reasons the philosophy of time has enjoyed such a resurgence in recent decades is due to the revolutionary findings of twentieth century physics. Einstein's theories of relativity shed a bright new light on these old problems, and it is to this physics that we now turn.

2 The Physics of Spacetime

Physics uses mathematical formalism and observational data to formulate laws (or describe regularities) that determine the behaviour of objects, events, and their relations with each other. This requires a fixed system within which the relevant entities can be described. To do this, one assigns coordinates to events and objects, and all events and objects that are stationary relative to each other and moving with uniform velocity comprise a so-called *inertial frame of reference*. Inertial motion occurs when force-free bodies move in straight lines at uniform velocity. If two bodies are in such motion relative to each other, meaning they are both moving in straight lines at uniform velocity relative to each other, then they can be described within the same inertial frame. There are an infinite number of frames of reference, as the starting point for one's coordinate system can be chosen arbitrarily. These frames are an integral conceptual tool when understanding physics' treatment of space, time, and motion.

Investigation into the nature of space and time using something like the modern scientific method began with Isaac Newton. Most famously, Newton developed his theory of gravitation and three laws of motion. Each of these was held to be universal, meaning they applied in every inertial frame. In Newtonian mechanics, one typically assumes that space is a receptacle in which objects and events exist, and that time passes uniformly. In *Philosophiae Naturalis Principia Mathematica,* Newton argues that 'absolute, true, and mathematical time, of itself, and from its own nature, flows equably without relation to anything external, and by another name is called duration' (Newton: Scholium to Definition viii). Both time and space are absolutes, regardless of whether we are able to accurately measure them as such, and both exist independently of the entities they contain. Hence, Newton endorsed substantivalism (interestingly, also for theological reasons).

Against this intellectual backdrop he developed his laws of motion. The phenomenon of true motion was understood as the movement of a body through absolute space in absolute time. Each is understood as independent of, and in opposition to, relative time, relative space, and relative motion, as these are determined by our measurements of them. Whilst we might measure the relative motion of a bicycle against a pavement, true motion requires the existence of absolute space which functions as a privileged reference frame. Newton developed several thought experiments to argue in favour of this (Maudlin 2012: chapter 2).

So, Newton maintained that time flows at a uniform rate everywhere in the universe and that this temporal metric is independent of the contingencies of any physical processes one might use as a clock. From these follow a commitment to the existence of an absolute simultaneity relation that holds between distant events. In effect, a single time value can be assigned to every slice of time that passes in the whole universe, and it is meaningful to assign the same time coordinate to events at either side of the universe. As we shall see, Special Relativity profoundly violated these assumptions.

2.1 Special Relativity

The Special Theory of Relativity (henceforth SR) was developed in response to a crisis in physics. This crisis was wrought by the infamous null result of the 1887 Michelson–Morley experiment, which was devised to test the luminiferous aether hypothesis. Two of light's properties contributed to the hypothesis of the luminiferous aether (an all-pervasive light-bearing medium) the first of which is its speed, and the second is its wave-like nature. With regard to the former, one can derive from Maxwell's equations that the speed of light in a vacuum is a constant, denoted as c. As the speed of light is constant, physicists postulated that there must be some background structure against which the fixity of this speed could be measured. The latter draws on the fact that light was believed to be a wave, and waves require a medium through which to propagate – sound waves cannot travel in a vacuum, and physicists believed this must also be the case for light waves.

Electromagnetic radiation (light) was believed to be a kind of stress in the aether analogous to stresses in solid, liquid, and gaseous materials that transmit sound waves. If the aether exists, then it would be a structure against which things have absolute motion, and motion through it should be detectable. In order to test this hypothesis, Albert Michelson and Edward Morley designed an experimental device which measured the speed of light in perpendicular directions, believing that the measured speeds would vary in accordance with the earth's motion through the aether. They did not detect any variation in the velocity of light, meaning that there was no detectable aether against which the fixity of c could be measured. Shockwaves reverberated throughout physics, and various attempts to save the aether theory were proposed. Ultimately, an explanation was offered in 1905 by a twenty-five-year-old patent clerk whose revolutionary ideas would change the landscape of physics forever. His name was Albert Einstein.

Einstein derived SR from two postulates. First is the *relativity principle*, which claims that the laws of physics are invariant between inertial frames. This means that the laws of physics do not change depending on whether an observer is stationary or in uniform motion. Second is the *light postulate*, whereby the speed of light in a vacuum is c irrespective of the speed of the source. In the Newtonian system, there is a tension between these two postulates, as velocity is cumulative. So, light emitted from a moving source should have the combined velocity of $c + v$ where v is the velocity of the source. Yet if the speed of light isn't always c, then there are certain observational perspectives from which a fundamental law of physics is broken, and the relativity principle is violated. Within Newtonian mechanics, these postulates cannot both be true.

It is by reconciling these two postulates that relativity's counterintuitive conclusions follow. The price is abandoning the Newtonian commitment to absolute time which passes at a uniform rate for all observers, and absolute space which acts as an unmoving and unchanging receptacle. How did Einstein arrive at this conclusion? Well, one calculates velocity by dividing the distance travelled by the amount of time that it takes: velocity = distance ÷ time.

To ensure that observers always agree that the speed of light in a vacuum is *c,* then they cannot always agree on either *time* or *distance.* Though this move is highly counter-intuitive, it is mathematically sound and has since been empirically verified to an extremely high degree of accuracy (Kennedy and Thorndike 1932; Ives and Stilwell 1938).

In other words, SR reveals that your measurements of distance, duration, and simultaneity will be dependent on your observational perspective (or, more technically, your reference frame). I will explain how this plays out through the use of a familiar example. Imagine two observers moving relative to each other. One (Raymond) is on a train travelling west to east, and the other (Pepe) sits on the train platform. Just as the train passes, two bolts of lightning strike: one a mile to the west and one a mile to the east. A very short time later, Pepe sees both flashes simultaneously. Knowing the distance to each strike, he concludes that the two strikes occurred simultaneously. But is he right?

Raymond does not observe both flashes simultaneously. Pepe thinks he has a simple explanation for Raymond's confusion: The light coming from the west had to catch up with Raymond, and Raymond is approaching the light coming from the east. This answer would work if you could say that Pepe is really at rest and Raymond is really in motion. But, according to SR, Raymond is just as justified in saying they were not simultaneous as Pepe is in saying that they were simultaneous. There is no feature of SR, or, as far as we know, any physical theory, that would allow us to say who is right and who is wrong. Each describes the situation from the standpoint of his frame of reference, and there is no authoritative, independent standpoint that could decide the matter. From this, we must conclude that simultaneity is relative.

It follows that an observer's measurement of temporal duration is frame-dependent. Indeed, experimental physicists have shown that highly accurate atomic clocks run at different rates when one is accelerated and the other remains stationary. This phenomenon, time dilation, is also frequently explained through the Twins' paradox. Here, one imagines that twins are separated, one remaining on Earth and the other accelerated to a significant fraction of the speed of light. The effect of motion on time (particularly as it approaches the speed of light) leads to the counterintuitive result that the Twins will be of different ages when they reunite.

These results can be explained geometrically by the unification of space and time into the more fundamental spacetime. Whilst one's measurement of time and space may vary, the spacetime interval between events is fixed. SR shows that two observers travelling at different velocities may get a different measurement for the distance and time between two events, but will agree on the spacetime interval. There are many ways to slice the spacetime interval pie into distances and durations, but no matter how the pie is sliced its total size does not change.

This is a direct consequence of Minkowski spacetime's luminal structure. Meaning, that the Minkowski metric uses the speed of light to determine the spatio-temporal distance between events, and relations between these events are dependent on *light cones*. Lightcones are divided into past lightcones and future lightcones. If a bulb goes off in a vacuum at some spatio-temporal location O, the light will occupy the entire future lightcone of O; O's past lightcone is comprised of all the light rays that reach point O. Lightcones draw out the connection between causality and light signals in SR – anything outside the past or future lightcone of O is causally unrelated to O, as there is no way a signal (or anything else, due to c's function as a cosmic speed limit) could reach O if it does not pass through O's lightcone.

Events within the past or future lightcone are called time-like separated from O, as reference frames may disagree about whether they are in the same location, but all reference frames agree that they occur at different times. Events on the future or past lightcone are light-like separated from O. Those outside the lightcone are space-like separated from O, as there may be disagreement between frames about whether they are simultaneous but there is no reference frame in which they are at the same location. Through spacetime diagrams, one can plot an observer's path (their worldline) through Minkowski spacetime and calculate the amount of time dilation and length contraction they would measure in the distance and time between events relative to another reference frame.

Coordinate systems and the reference frames they map are arbitrary devices used to represent observational perspectives, so moving between them without violating the laws of physics must be possible if the theory is to work. One calculates this move between inertial frames using the Lorentz transformations, as these are the only transformations that preserve the universality (i.e. non-frame-dependence) of the speed of light. This allows one to move between inertial reference frames without concluding that the observers within them have to disagree about invariant physical laws like the fixity of c. In preserving the fixity of the speed of light when moving from one inertial frame to another, one gets time dilation and/or length contraction, and thus a theoretical explanation for the relativity of simultaneity. Further details of the special theory are not within the scope of this work. The aforementioned is all we need to move forward with the philosophical and theological relevance of spacetime. For further reading, see (Bohm 2006; Baron and Miller 2019: chapter 4).

There have been several interpretations of SR, but by far the most widely held is the so-called spacetime interpretation (or, Einstein-Minkowski interpretation).

Here, SR is taken as disclosing ontological facts about time and space and, importantly, as holding that no claims can be made about the nature of either except those contained within the theory. The spacetime interpretation is grounded on operationalist principles, a point of contention amongst critics. The Operationalist defines scientific concepts in terms of the operations used to demonstrate them, maintaining that meaning is inextricably linked to measurement. For example, an operational definition of time would be that time is that which is measured by clocks (Einstein 2010 [1920]: 22). With regards to SR, our failure to measure absolute simultaneity means that absolute simultaneity does not exist. The spacetime interpretation, then, is committed to the following: (1) space and time are distinct dimensions of the more fundamental entity *spacetime*, (2) absolute simultaneity relations do not exist within the special theory because they do not exist in the world, (3) one's measurement of duration and length is determined by one's frame of reference. But what does this mean metaphysically?

The A-theory requires the existence of an objective, changing, universal *now* at which point potential future events *come into being* when they become present. If the present cannot be clearly defined, then it cannot be an ontologically privileged boundary between the actual present and the potential future. Yet following SR we know that some events (specifically, spacelike separated events) that are future in one reference frame might be present in another, meaning 'future' events already exist. This argument was most famously made by Hilary Putnam (Putnam 1967: 242). Almost every A-theory is committed to a non-actualised future, and all are committed to an objective *now*. The spacetime interpretation of SR seems incompatible with these claims. Thus, the spacetime interpretation follows either a B-theory or C-theory of time. This is also referred to as a four-dimensional spacetime ontology as it unites the three dimensions of space with the one dimension of time.

A well-known alternative is the neo-Lorentzian interpretation championed by William Lane Craig. Craig is a committed presentist who has devoted much of his career to defending the A-theory through his contributions to a wide variety of philosophical and theological debates. There are three key points in his argument. The first is a commitment to the existence of some form of background structure which functions as a preferred frame of reference. Against this preferred frame of reference, the objective passage of time can be measured, and absolute simultaneity relations can be substantiated. Craig suggests a range of possibilities that might replace the defunct luminiferous aether (Craig 2001: 165). We will examine one such proposal in the next section.

The second component of Craig's argument invokes the Newtonian distinction between absolute, metaphysical, time on the one hand, and relative, physical time on the other. He argues that time dilation and length contraction are only consequences of relative, measured, time and space. Our inability to empirically access absolute, metaphysical, time is a consequence of our methodological limitations and not of absolute time's non-existence. The omniscient God knows which events are simultaneous in the universal *now* of metaphysical time, even if we limited creatures do not (and, indeed, cannot). On this view, SR describes physical processes, leaving the metaphysical time (grounded in divine time) untouched. Hence, an A-theory can be preserved despite the empirical evidence against absolute simultaneity and a global now. Or so the argument goes. The third point is the importance of theism in motivating the neo-Lorentzian position. Craig argues that God must be temporal for theological reasons (see Section 3.1), and a temporal God only makes sense in a universe in which time flows. It is for this reason that Craig endorses presentism, arguing that theists cannot accept block universe interpretations of scientific theories and must seek alternative, A-theoretic, interpretations. This position is often referred to as a 3+1 spacetime ontology, as it is committed to a clear distinction between three-dimensional space and one-dimensional time. A third, also A-theoretic, interpretation of SR has been proposed by Robert John Russell (2012, 2022). Russell names his interpretation the *inhomogeneous flowing time* interpretation, discussion of which unfortunately falls outside the scope of this Element.

Whilst SR is perhaps the most directly relevant physical theory when it comes to the issue of spacetime, it does not have the last word. SR only applies in the world of flat spacetime and inertial frames, leaving gravitation and accelerating frames out of the picture. For a more comprehensive understanding of spacetime and how it interacts with matter, we must turn to the General Theory of Relativity.

2.2 General Relativity

In 1915 Einstein published the application of SR to gravitational fields, his crowning achievement, the General Theory of Relativity (henceforth GR). GR superseded Newton's explanation of gravity, ushering in an entirely new understanding of space, time, and the interactions between objects within them. Newtonian mechanics described gravity as a force holding between objects that is directly proportional to the product of their masses and inversely proportional to the square of the distance between their centres. Einsteinian GR, on the other hand, described gravity as the warping of the four-dimensional fabric of spacetime by massive bodies.

One can visualise how this works by imagining a sheet held taught at each corner with a bowling ball in the centre. The bowling ball will warp the sheet, effecting the motion of any objects rolling past it. A ping pong ball rolled near the bowling ball will have its trajectory altered; in fact, it may begin rolling around the bowling ball as though it is in orbit. Similarly, gravity is not a force that holds between entities, rather it is a consequence of the warping of the spacetime in which these entities dwell. Whilst the analogy with a sheet and balls is an imperfect representation insofar as it lacks a third spatial dimension, the general principle is the same. As John Wheeler pithily put it, spacetime tells matter how to move, and matter tells spacetime how to curve.

The warping of spacetime does not only affect the motion of celestial bodies like stars and galaxies. Observers will measure different durations between two events closer to a massive body than observers in the vacuum of space. One can understand why when considering the fixity of the speed of light. Light always takes the shortest path between two points. In flat spacetime, this is a straight line. If spacetime is curved, then light will be travelling a greater distance along the curvature of spacetime than it will where spacetime is flatter. The 'straight line' in curved spacetime is known as a *geodesic*. In GR, light follows spacetime geodesics, and the greater the curvature of spacetime the greater the distance light must travel. Observers in a reference frame in which spacetime exhibits significant curvature must still measure the speed of light as c, just as observers in a reference frame where spacetime is not so curved will. Because speed = distance ÷ time, these observers will disagree on the duration between given events. So, an astronaut could be on a massive planet for an hour in their time, but on returning to their spaceship they could find that their colleagues who remained on the ship had measured twenty years between the astronaut leaving and returning. You may have seen this phenomenon depicted in science fiction films.

Despite the theoretically sound and empirically substantiated effects of gravitational time dilation, some philosophers have argued that the case for dynamic time is significantly improved within GR. Both Richard Swinburne and William Lane Craig have argued that certain solutions of Einstein's field equations, each of which corresponds to a possible world, can substantiate a privileged 'cosmic time'. They argue that this re-awakens the plausibility of an absolute present moment, and hence an A-theory of time (Swinburne 2008: 224).

The solutions in question are Friedman–Lemaître–Robertson–Walker (henceforth FLRW) cosmological solutions of GR, each of which corresponds to a possible universe structure. FLRW universes possess the following properties: (1) homogeneity (the universe is the same at every point); (2) isotropy (there is no preferred direction in the universe); (3) expansion (the overall size of the universe evolves dynamically). These symmetries mean that one can foliate spacetime in such a way that globally extended instants, that is, universal *nows*, emerge. This time parameter is called 'cosmic time', and if it is a feature of the physical world then the A-theory may be saved.

Swinburne argues that one can relegate SR's inability to substantiate absolute simultaneity relations to one of measurement and not ontology. Meaning, the A-theory's chances in GR are substantially improved. The symmetries in an FLRW universe allow spacetime to be foliated into absolute simultaneity planes that substantiate cosmic simultaneity and thus cosmic time. Such time charts the passage of time since the beginning of the universe in an observer-independent way, that is, without having to account for variability between moving frames, rendering the A-theorist's absolute present coherent within physics once again. Swinburne fleshes these claims out with an argument for the A-theory that relies on a thought experiment seeking to operationally access cosmic time (which is unfortunately misguided) and an assertion that our universe is indeed an FLRW universe (which is an open empirical question).

Critiques of this strategy are multifarious. First, one might argue that focusing on cosmological solutions of GR changes the theory under consideration, illegitimately disengaging from the relevant domain of discourse. Second, one might object that cosmological solutions of GR are mere idealisations and are therefore not true descriptions of the actual world. A third response is to argue that using cosmic simultaneity as a vehicle for grounding an objective past/present/future distinction is ill-conceived. The original motivation to introduce an A-theory was to recover our experience of temporal passage. Yet cosmic time is radically disconnected from that experience, so it cannot establish the kind of temporal passage the A-theorist requires. Finally, one might follow Gödel in presenting a modal argument to the effect that whether a universe manifests primitive tensed properties cannot be a contingent affair. Since (for technical reasons) it would have to be a contingent affair in GR, there can exist no such objective tensed properties. Each of these is explored in greater detail in Read and Qureshi-Hurst (2021).

Although the A-theory invariably fares better in GR than SR, there are a multitude of arguments that encourage hesitancy about absolute simultaneity, and thus the A-theory, in GR. The block universe remains the most plausible temporal ontology in a relativistic context. Nevertheless, both GR and SR are incomplete theories – it is only after a Quantum Theory of Gravity emerges that we might hope to have further answers to some of our most significant questions about the nature of spatio-temporal reality.

2.3 Quantum Gravity

One of the biggest problems in physics today is that its two most successful theories are presently incompatible. As we have seen, GR describes the large-scale behaviour of celestial bodies like stars and galaxies. Quantum Mechanics (henceforth QM) describes the small-scale behaviour of sub-atomic particles. Whilst the sources of their incompatibility are multifarious, two are of interest here. First, in GR spacetime is continuous, meaning it is smooth and infinitely divisible (essentially, between any two spacetime points there is a third). QM, however, introduces granularity into myriad properties at the sub-atomic level, such as energy and length. These properties can only have certain values, functions of Plank's constant, meaning that there is a minimum value below which they cannot go. A quantum theory of gravity, namely a theory uniting GR and QM, is needed to understand whether gravity, and therefore spacetime, is continuous or particulate.

Second, absolute simultaneity plays an important role in QM. Non-relativistic QM currently has several viable interpretations. In all interpretations, however, an absolute spacetime structure is taken for granted and Newtonian-style absolute time is used to mark the evolution of a quantum system. Interactions between entangled quantum particles great distances apart are faster than the speed of light, seeming to require instantaneous (thus absolutely simultaneous) spooky-action-at-a-distance of the kind forbidden by relativity. The GRW interpretation also employs simultaneity when specifying how the wavefunction collapses, and Bohmian mechanics requires an absolute temporal structure to guide the pilot wave (Maudlin 2019: 205–6). Regardless of interpretation, QM appears to require absolute time of the kind that cannot be substantiated in either GR or SR. As Edward Anderson explains, 'time is a general spacetime coordinate in GR, clashing with ordinary QM's having held time to be a unique and sui generis extraneous quantity' (Anderson 2012: 759). This is the so-called 'problem of time' in quantum gravity. How can these two mutually incompatible descriptions of time be reconciled?

Despite Quantum Field Theory's incorporation of special relativistic considerations (regarding particles nearing the speed of light) a unification of QM and GR, namely a quantum theory of gravity, remains an ultimate goal of theoretical physics. That such a theory is yet to be found is partially due to difficulties with developing the formalism, and partly because of limitations with our technical ability to test these theory's predictions at the extremely small scales required. Some approaches seek to quantise spacetime, bringing gravity in line with the three other fundamental forces described by the standard model of particle physics. Some approaches are more radical, arguing that spacetime is emergent and that we should forget time altogether when working in the quantum realm. Others have gone as far as to argue that a quantum theory of gravity will lack any temporal metric at all, and will thus be a genuinely timeless theory. Ultimately, the jury is still out on what a unification of GR and QM would mean for temporal metaphysics and the physics of spacetime. If we want physics to solve our philosophical uncertainties about time, then we must wait. With all the philosophical and physical landscape set out, we are now able to proceed to theological questions.

3 God and Time

Why should theists care about all this? Well, almost all Christian theologians agree that God is without beginning or end, and that this is an essential attribute of the divine personhood (Wolterstorff and Cuneo 2010: 133). Whether this property should be understood as eternal (i.e. timeless, outside of time) or everlasting (i.e. temporal, exists at all times), is a core theological question. Theists should also care about the metaphysics and physics of time because these seek to describe a fundamental feature of creation. Many important theological issues are related to the nature of time, as these concern the relation between creature and creator. The foci of this section are those questions most frequently discussed in the literature: is God within time, experiencing passage as the history of creation unfolds? Or is God outside of time, able to view all tenselessly existing moments at once? As will become clear in the subsequent discussion, much of this debate hangs on one's prior commitments, theological priorities, and which model of God's relationship to time is most coherent with these.

3.1 God as Atemporal

If God is atemporal, or timeless, then God does not exist within time (i.e. have temporal location, extension, or parts), experience any temporal phenomenon such as passage or succession, or enter into any temporal relations. Nor does God have a beginning or end. Additionally, following Boethius, the atemporalist understands God to have 'complete possession all at once of illimitable life', meaning God's life is not comprised of temporal parts and is instead held together in one eternal present. The idea of God as timeless has a rich and enduring history (Section 1.2). Until very recently, divine atemporality was accepted by an overwhelming majority of theologians and philosophers of religion stretching at least as far back as the patristic period. The Church Fathers, who worked to establish theological orthodoxy in the emerging Church, frequently turned to their Greek forebears to provide the philosophical framework within which key Christian doctrines were to be articulated. As such, from late antiquity to the high medieval period, Christian theology was influenced by Plato's writings, especially regarding doctrines of God. It is within this context that several atemporalist arguments emerge.

One argument for a timeless God is based on the Platonic idea of divine immutability. Immutability combines elements of Plato's ontology of the Forms which are perfect, immaterial, and unchanging, with perfect being theology which holds that God is a supremely perfect being. In Republic (381b-c), Plato argued that a perfect being cannot change, as they can neither improve (as they are already perfect) nor degenerate (as any change would be a degradation from perfection). Thus, a perfect God must be immutable. This conclusion had a profound influence on Christian tradition. Following Aristotle's commitment to the inextricable link between time and change, an immutable being was believed to be outside of time by necessity. Such a God does not gain or lose any properties, nor any parts of his life; he does not have to wait for a distant future or lose something precious into the vanishing past. For these reasons, it is theologically appealing. But does it cohere with other, perhaps equally important, theological claims?

There are several ways one might critique this argument, two of which I will consider here. First, the argument assumes that there is only one way to be perfect. Perhaps this idea was rooted in Platonic ideas about the Form of the Good being the single, ultimate, perfect, immaterial, and immutable realisation of goodness. However, it is an assumption for which inadequate justification is given. It is not clear, for example, how a change in God's knowledge of what time it is, say from 3:00 pm to 3:01 pm, constitutes a deviation from perfection. If these changes have no effect on a being's perfection, then the argument from perfection to immutability is undermined. Second, one could critique the claim that God does not change by referring to Scriptural passages that show God dynamically interacting with human affairs as and when they transpire. One of many examples of this is God's interaction with Moses at the burning bush (Exodus 3). Nicholas Wolterstorff argues that such passages indicate that God is involved in the narratives that shape human history, and that he has a personal interest in acting in and responding to temporal creation. This signifies both that God changes, and that God is within time (Wolterstorff and Cuneo 2010: chapter 8).

Some atemporalists make a parallel argument, focusing instead on divine simplicity. Traditionally, God is understood as perfectly simple, meaning he is not composed of parts (temporal or otherwise). According to Brian Leftow's reconstruction of Aquinas, an entity is only temporal if it satisfies one or more of the following criteria: (1) it can change intrinsically, (2) it can change its place, (3) it has parts which can change places, (4) it can begin or cease to exist. A being with no parts (temporal or otherwise), who does not begin or cease to exist, is not a temporal being. As God is perfectly simple and does not satisfy any of these criteria, he is not a temporal being (Leftow 2005: 62; Deng 2019a: 36).

The atemporalist can also draw on God's sovereignty and omnipotence. The former property refers to God being the ultimate ruler of creation who is radically free to act in accordance with his own will. The latter refers to God's supreme powerfulness. If God is both omnipotent and sovereign, then God is not subservient to any force, process, or external influence of any kind. Rather, God is the all-powerful creator and supreme ruler of creation and is free to engage with that creation in any way he so chooses. Yet if time passes and God is within time, then God must be subject to temporal passage as would any other temporal being. A temporal God cannot directly experience any moment except that which is present, radically limiting divine omnipotence and making God subordinate to the external and relentless march of time. If God were subject to the passage of time in this way, then atemporalists argue that he would be time's prisoner. This is an unacceptable conclusion if one wishes God to remain both omnipotent and sovereign. We will explore responses to this objection in Section 3.2.

A final theological argument for divine atemporality is based on the interwoven issues of omniscience, freedom, and foreknowledge. Classical theism holds that God is omniscient, meaning that God knows all that it is logically possible to know. Christianity, however, also places significant emphasis on the importance of libertarian freedom, defined as the freedom to choose between more than one genuinely viable option. If you are free in a libertarian sense, you are able to choose between (for example) having toast or cereal for breakfast tomorrow, and until you make that choice tomorrow morning, these are both genuinely viable options. If you had wanted to have something different for breakfast this morning, you could have done so..

Such freedom is essential for the notions of moral and soteriological responsibility, for it seems utterly unjust to hold humans responsible for choices that they did not freely make. The problem, then, is as follows: God cannot know what you will decide to do tomorrow without taking away your libertarian freedom. For if God knows that you will eat toast tomorrow, and he is omniscient, then his knowing that you will eat toast entails that you will eat toast. Cereal was never actually an option you could choose. If God does not know what you will eat tomorrow, however, then God's omniscience is challenged. If there is a fact about what you will eat tomorrow, namely if the statement 'you eat toast tomorrow' is true, then an omniscient God must know it. So, it looks like the temporalist must eschew one of these incompatible claims. Either we are not free, or God is not omniscient. This is known as the problem of divine foreknowledge and human freedom.

The atemporalist can solve this problem by saying that God is outside of time, able to view all events at once, and so God *atemporally knows* what you will have for breakfast tomorrow because elsewhere in the block universe (the temporal model that goes hand in hand with the atemporal God) it *is* tomorrow, and you *are* eating it. God knows and sees all moments of creation from the divine atemporal perspective. He does not know what you will do *before* you do it, because an atemporal God does not enter into temporal relations with temporal beings. Proponents argue that atemporal knowledge, thus defined, does not affect libertarian freedom, and so solves the problem of divine fore-knowledge and human freedom. Whether this actually solves the problem is a matter of contention. See the *Cambridge Element* in *God and Time* for further discussion (Deng 2019a: 37–8).

The temporalist can respond to this problem also, via the position known as *Open Theism*. Open Theism refers back to the (reasonable) caveat that God's omniscience means that God knows everything *that it is logically possible to know*. Open Theists affirm an A-theory of time in which the future is non-existent, such as presentism or the growing block, and reject determinism whereby there is a single fixed future at t' determined by (the laws of nature) + (the state of the world at some time t). On this view, the future is epistemically *and* ontologically open, and until the abstract, non-real future becomes the concrete, real present, there are propositions about that future which do not have a truth value. Free agents have genuine choices about which actions to take, and these choices make material differences to which potential future states of affairs are actualised.

Open Theists, then, deny that there are any facts of the future that an omniscient being could know, except perhaps regularities like the rising sun or theological assertions such as God's promises will be fulfilled. Thus, both divine omniscience and libertarian freedom are preserved on Open Theism. As with any theological position, one might have reasonable reservations about this view, particularly with regard to the level of risk God takes by creating a world over whose direction he has limited control. It is theoretic-ally possible, on Open Theism, for God to create a world in which no free being enters into a relationship with him, a very undesirable possibility for the theist indeed.

Another route one might take when defending divine timelessness is to follow Brian Leftow in arguing for the position for relativistic reasons. Leftow writes:

(1) God is an immaterial substance.
(2) Immaterial substances are not in space. So,
(3) God is not in space. . . . But,
(4) according to relativity theory, anything that is in time is also in space.

Therefore,

(5) if relativity theory is correct (in essentials), then God is not in time.

(6) Relativity theory is correct (in essentials). So,

(7) God is not in time. So,

(8) God is timeless. (Leftow 1991: 272)

Special Relativity's unification of space and time into the more fundamental spacetime leads to the conclusion that something cannot be spatial but not temporal (or *vice versa*), and, if a transcendent non-corporeal God cannot be spatial, he cannot be temporal either. Of course, such an argument only works on the spacetime interpretation of relativity that holds a four-dimensional spacetime ontology. Craig's neo-Lorentzian 3+1 spacetime ontology frees up the temporal dimension enough to allow God to be within time but not with space. However, as neo-Lorentzianism fails for other reasons (see Balashov and Janssen 2003), Leftow's argument from relativity remains compelling.

The atemporal God–time relational model makes most sense on a B-theory or C-theory of time, whereby reality is comprised of a block universe and an eternal God views all the tenselessly existent events in creation from an atemporal, external perspective. On this view, God does not experience passage or presentness because these properties do not exist anywhere in time or eternity. Rather, God directly apprehends the block universe in its entirety from an atemporal perspective, as a reader may hold all the events of a novel in their hand at once. Accordingly, divine omniscience, sovereignty, immutability, perfection, and transcendence are preserved. Nevertheless, problems are posed for God's ability to respond dynamically to the unfolding of creation (including responding to petitionary prayer) and divine immanence. It is also unclear how an atemporal God could enter temporal creation in the Incarnation. We now turn to the alternative view: divine temporality.

3.2 God as Temporal

When a theist states that God is temporal, they are claiming that God is within time, subject to its passage, and thus experiences the unfolding of world history as it occurs. God is everlasting, existing at every moment of created time, rather than eternal, existing outside of time altogether. The writer of Psalm 102:23–28, for example, says of God:

Long ago you laid the foundation of the earth, and the heavens are the work of your hands. They will perish, but you endure; they will all wear out like a garment. You change them like clothing, and they pass away; but you are the same, and your years have no end.

Wolterstorff argues that this is scriptural evidence that God endures everlasting. God has years, and thus he is temporal, but, unlike the transitory years of finite creatures, they have no end (Wolterstorff and Cuneo 2010: 162). Temporalists may also be claiming that God occupies certain spatio-temporal locations (i.e. God is present everywhere in physical reality), although these views are distinct and should be treated as such.

Temporalists also draw upon the idea that God is a person with a history and with whom we can enter into a relationship. Relationships require some form of interaction between two parties, and this interaction can be said to have a narrative structure. This involves participants evolving together in an ongoing relationship, seemingly requiring each to be temporal and thus able to change in response to, and in dialogue with, the other. Wolterstorff argues that 'God has a history, and in this history there are changes in God's actions, responses, and knowledge' (Wolterstorff and Cuneo 2010: 158). Furthermore, Christianity teaches that God-the-Son took on human flesh to become a temporal person. If the Father, Son, and Spirit are wholly and equally God then this is a fairly compelling argument for divine temporality, as it is hard to imagine how one of the Trinitarian persons can have a distinct temporal mode to any of the others (Holland 2012).

Wolterstorff grounds his view in Scriptural depictions of God as an agent with interests in, and contextual knowledge of, historical situations (which changes with the changing situation), and as a being who interacts with creation in a deeply personal way. The Bible does not portray a detached, atemporal God. Instead, the Bible bears witness to a God who cares about human affairs and is intentionally embedded in the historical narratives that shape human existence. These ideas only make sense on a non-eternalist A-theory which holds to the reality of newness, becoming, and change. A block universe already contains all the objects and events that will ever exist – it is a closed system that cannot accommodate action from outside.

Therefore, the temporal view of God is usually held in concordance with an A-theory of time – God experiences temporal phenomena like passage because time does really pass; God responds dynamically to time because time itself is dynamic, and so on. Many of the advantages of divine temporality require an A-theory of time, thus arguing for the A-theory is a popular refrain amongst temporalists. For example, William Lane Craig argues at length that an A-theory is the only theologically plausible theory of time (Craig 2001: 165). Robert John Russell agrees with Craig that we need an A-theory of time for theological reasons (Russell 2012: 308). Ryan Mullins even goes as far as to claim that all classical theists are really presentists and that the doctrine of divine timelessness should be permanently discarded (Mullins 2016: chapter 4).

Whilst the fine-structure of God's relationship with temporal creation depends on whether one subscribes to presentism, the growing block theory, the moving spotlight view, or some other A-theory, all temporalists agree that God is within time, God knows what time it is *now*, and that created temporality is importantly dependent on divine temporality. Absolute simultaneity, for example, is substantiated in the mind of God and not (or not only) in the physical relations between objects and events. Although variation exists within advocates of a temporal God, it is fair to say that an overwhelming majority are presentists. Interestingly, presentism is a minority view in most other philosophical circles, especially philosophy of physics. Perhaps this is because most reasons given for endorsing presentism are theological, rather than purely metaphysical or scientific.

Woven throughout theological arguments for an A-theory of time are concerns about divine omniscience and tensed facts. One such argument runs as follows. There are certain things about A-series time, namely tensed facts, that one can only know if one is subject to the dynamic unfolding of events. An example of which is what time it is now. These facts change with the passage of time, so God's knowledge must change too. If God's knowledge changes, then God changes, and if God changes then he is a temporal being. God also changes as he sustains each new moment of time which becomes present and then disappears into the vanishing past. So, God, on this view, is not immutable (at least in a strong sense) and must be within time. Moreover, if a being is outside A-series time, then they experience neither nowness nor passage – something Delmas Lewis terms 'actuality-blindness' (Lewis 1984: 78). But if these are central features of creation, then an omniscient being must know them. See Deng (2019a: 42–6) for an in-depth discussion of various versions of this argument and its connection to temporal metaphysics.

The atemporalist may object on the grounds that sacrificing divine simplicity and immutability to preserve God's changing knowledge is too high a price to pay. The problem is serious, they argue, as on the most popular A-theory, presentism, time objectively passes and only the present exists. God is forced to experience the tenses as they objectively occur. God cannot go back to the past except in memory, and, as long as individuals have some genuine freedom, God is unable to know the future (in so far as that future is pure potentiality, as yet unshaped by the free choices of agents). God cannot experience or interact with anything other than the present, as on presentism nothing else exists. This renders almost all of creation utterly inaccessible to God, making the challenge to divine sovereignty and omnipotence profound.

This leads to a popular critique of divine temporality known as the 'prisoner of time' objection: if God is within the boundaries of time, then he must be subservient to it. In other words, time stands over and above God who is subject to the inexorability of its passing. God cannot break free of the relentless march of time, and so is a prisoner whose omnipotence and sovereignty is undermined. Richard Swinburne responds to this objection by arguing that God is inside time, but, crucially, by choice. Therefore, no challenge to divine omnipotence is raised. Swinburne argues that effects cannot precede, or be simultaneous with, their causes. Causes must always precede their effects. Yet for God to be outside time he would have to be simultaneous with the creation of the universe and every subsequent event within it (except events that are the result of free human agency), meaning that divine causality would be simultaneous with its effects. As this is a logical impossibility, Swinburne argues, the timeless understanding of God is incoherent (Swinburne 1993). It is for this reason that Swinburne argues that God *chooses* to be inside time. God has good reason to make such a choice: (1) to achieve a level of intimacy with creation that could not otherwise have been achieved, and (2) to be able to respond to petitionary prayer. He willingly sacrifices some sovereignty, but as this was a free choice God remains both omnipotent and sovereign. (Swinburne 1993.

Ryan Mullins constructs an alternative response to the prisoner of time objection, arguing that it rests on a mischaracterisation of the divine temporalist's view. The prisoner of time objection assumes that time is separate to God, and thus that God cannot escape time's passing in the same way that we humans are subject to the external force of gravity that keeps us securely on the Earth. Mullins argues that this is a mistake. Whilst such a view would challenge divine sovereignty, this is not the temporalist's view. Instead, time should be thought of as a 'necessary concomitant of [the divine] being' (Mullins 2014: 165). On this view, God should be thought of as weakly immutable, meaning that whilst his essential attributes do not change, he can undergo non-essential changes such as becoming the creator, redeemer, and Lord of humanity. Since God is a necessary being, and God undergoes such change, then time (required for change) exists necessarily.

Mullins argues that the very fact that God creates time shows that it is not some external force imprisoning him. Quite the opposite, in fact. God chooses to create both time and beings who live within that time in order that he can enter into covenantal relationships with those beings. In so doing, God willingly takes temporal properties like succession into his life, along with all the benefits these bring. Divine sovereignty emerges unscathed because it is defined as God's ability to perfectly realise his ultimate purposes for the creation that he chooses to bring into being. This can be achieved whilst being within time.

Temporalist and presentist William Lane Craig holds a similar view, arguing that God exists changelessly and timelessly prior to creation and then in time once creation has been brought into being (Craig 1999: 522). The claim that God is creatively active in the temporal world, he argues, is absolutely essential to Christian theism. In order for God to know tensed facts, to experience things coming into being, and to respond directly to the wants and needs of creation, God must be temporal. Yet according to Craig, 'before' creating the universe, God cannot have been temporal, as there is no time without physical creation. For this reason, Craig maintains that God becomes temporal once he has created the universe.

Puzzlingly, Craig distinguishes between physical created time and metaphysical divine time. This distinction is necessary to get neo-Lorentzian relativity (and other such arguments for a temporal A-theory) over the line. 'Before' creation, God is timeless, which can only mean there is no metaphysical divine time. After creation God is temporal, meaning metaphysical divine time and physical time exist. But if God's time is not reducible to physical time (a core claim of neo-Lorentzian relativity), then why did God's metaphysical time come into being only after God created the universe and physical time (/spacetime)? If these two times are conceptually distinct, and metaphysical time is grounded in the mind of God, then it is not clear why such time becomes a feature of God's life only after physical time is created. Moreover, it is not easy to make sense of the idea that God becomes temporal after creating the universe – if God was in a 'before' (i.e. a temporal) relation with his creating the universe, then surely he has been temporal all along? Craig acknowledges this latter concern but never provides a fully satisfying response.

As is evident from the above, there are a multitude of conflicting perspectives about God's relation to time that tend to be split along A-theory/temporalist and B-theory/atemporalist lines. A third way has been proposed, however, that aims to combine an A-theory with atemporality. The proponents of this third way suggest a new relation between eternity and temporality that would allow an atemporal God to be actively present in a dynamic temporal creation. To such a proposal we now turn.

3.3 A Middle Way?

A much-debated way of conceiving of the God-time relation, developed by Eleonore Stump and Norman Kretzmann in the 1980s, is the so-called *Eternal-Temporal simultaneity relation* (henceforth E-T simultaneity). Stump and Kretzmann defended the doctrine of divine eternity whilst suggesting a route by which the downsides of eternity listed above, particularly those of divine inaccessibility and impersonality, can be avoided. In this way, their approach can be thought of as a middle way between the detached divine temporality of the medieval period and the intimate divine temporality that has risen to prominence in recent years. If it works, then it seems as though theists can have their metaphysical cake and eat it too – God would be atemporal and eternal *a la* tradition whilst retaining the ability to be intimately involved in a dynamic creation as it unfolds (as many modern theologians argue is essential).

Stump and Kretzmann's E-T simultaneity relation is intended to establish a link between two distinct modes of real existence: divine eternity and created temporality. They adopt a Boethian understanding of divine eternity in which God is outside of time. They also assume an absolute, Newtonian, and A-theoretic temporal present, and claim this is essential to their argument (Stump and Kretzmann 1981: 437, 440). Stump and Kretzmann begin by investigating the prima facie incoherence in combining elements of Boethian eternity in the divine being: atemporality on the one hand, and infinite duration and life on the other. Duration appears to be an inescapably temporal phenomenon, so how can we understand a life of atemporal, infinite, duration?

First, the events in an eternal being's life cannot be ordered successively, for they are possessed all at once. Nor can a temporal event be in any relation of *before* or *after* with the life of an eternal entity, as that would enter the eternal entity into a temporal series. The eternal entity exists in a single, eternal present that is quite unlike any fleeting temporal present flanked by past and future that we might experience. Instead, an eternal being always exists presently in an 'infinitely extended, pastless, futureless duration', none of their life is yet to come and none of it has passed away (Stump and Kretzmann 1981: 435, 445).

From this formulation of eternity, Stump and Kretzmann develop E-T simultaneity, defining simultaneity *simpliciter* as existence or occurrence at once (together). Two temporal events are simultaneous if they occur at the same time; two eternal events are simultaneous if they occur in the same eternal present. Yet this understanding of simultaneity will not work for relating events that occupy distinct modes of being. E-T simultaneity transcends the boundaries between eternality and temporality by combining (1) T-simultaneity, namely two or more events existing or occurring at the same *time*, and (2) E-simultaneity, namely existence or occurrence at one and the same *eternal present*. Reference frames are essential in making sense of simultaneity (both temporal and E-T). Just as physicists rely on the concept of a reference frame to denote an observer's observational perspective within spacetime, so too do Stump and Kretzmann need the concept to denote the perspective of an entity in the eternal present. E-T simultaneity is defined as follows:

(ET) For every x and for every y, x and y are ET-simultaneous iff

(i)   either x is eternal and y is temporal, or vice versa; and
(ii) for some observer, A, in the unique eternal reference frame, x and y are both present-i.e., either x is eternally present and y is observed as temporally present, or vice versa; and

(iii)   for some observer, B, in one of the infinitely many temporal reference frames, x and y are both present- i.e., either x is observed as eternally present and y is temporally present, or vice versa. (Stump and Kretzmann 1981: 439)

Essentially, two events are E-T simultaneous if both are perceived as present by an observer in the eternal reference frame, or by a temporal observer. Through this simultaneity relation, an eternal being is simultaneous with every temporal event. Importantly, E-T simultaneity is neither transitive (as there are different domains for its relata) nor reflexive (as no being can be E-T simultaneous with themselves), so one is not forced to falsely conclude that all temporal events are simultaneous with each other by virtue of being simultaneous with the eternal present.

If this view is correct, there are several implications that follow. First, it preserves both divine eternity and divine immanence, by showing that the action of a timelessly eternal being can be simultaneous with an event in created time. God is fully realised at all times as each moment of time is simultaneous with the eternal present, and so is omnipresent. God has epistemic access to all moments of time, so is omniscient, and can act at any moment of time, so is omnipotent. So far, so good.

A problem arises, however, with the idea that eternal duration can be both infinite (viz. it extends without limit in all directions) and atemporal. Atemporality and infinite duration seem incompatible, as duration seems to be a fundamentally temporal concept. This has led some to argue that duration without extension or temporal parts is not duration at all. Alan Padgett argues that 'atemporal duration' is an oxymoron, as duration is by definition an interval of time (Padgett 1992: 67). Brian Leftow also writes that by claiming that atemporal duration cannot be divided into component parts, Stump and Kretzmann are describing something much more like a point with zero extension than an infinitely extending eternity (Leftow 1991: 128). William Lane Craig, too, notes various difficulties with claiming atemporal duration can convey anything more than metaphorical meaning (Craig 1985).

It is fair to say that the most significant difficulties with this view arise from the apparent confusion laying at the heart of Stump and Kretzmann's understanding of divine eternity as possessing the properties of atemporality and infinite duration. Stump and Kretzmann have responded to such criticisms by arguing that the specious present is another example of an extended, yet conceptually indivisible (so exhibits none of the typical features of extension), experienced present and therefore their proposal is not as extraordinary as some critics make out (Stump and Kretzmann 1992). Regrettably, there is no space to delve deeper into Stump and Kretzmann's proposal and its defences. I invite the reader to turn to the Cambridge Element in 'God and Time' to explore these issues further (Deng 2019a: chapter 3).

The previous sections have focused on the more general theological questions surrounding the meaning of divine eternity and the relationship between an eternal (or everlasting) God and temporal creation. These discussions have dominated the discourse on temporal questions in both 'philosophy of religion' and 'science and religion'. Another set of fascinating and important conversations has been emerging in recent years that engages specific scientific theories concerning the nature of time and/or spacetime with particular theological doctrines. It is here that the problem of spacetime for salvation and eschatology emerges.

4 Spacetime, Salvation, and Eschatology

Everything in the previous discussion has been leading us to this point. The metaphysical groundwork has been laid, various interpretations of the nature and structure of spacetime have been set out, and some ways God might relate to that spacetime have been explored. This leads us to two problems for the interrelated doctrines of salvation and eschatology. The first problem I will consider relates to personal salvation, particularly the nature of change involved therein, and emerges on a block universe interpretation of spacetime (i.e. a B-theory or C-theory of time). This understanding of spatio-temporal reality is prima facie incompatible with the type of change required for personal salvation insofar as that salvation requires a transformation in time. I explore this problem in Section 4.1. The second problem arises from an A-theory of time (specifically presentism) and is one of eschatology. If GR is correct, then the universe will come to an end, meaning there will be a final event after which the universe's story is over. On presentism, this universal end is particularly troublesome as it would involve the total, irreversible destruction of the universe and its contents. If Christian eschatology requires both that the physical stuff of creation be transformed into a new creation and the physical bodies of saved individuals be resurrected, then the end of the universe is very bad news indeed.

A serious problem is raised for either salvation or eschatology by both of the two most successful ways of understanding the nature of spacetime. The former problem emerges from a four-dimensional spacetime ontology, the latter problem emerges from a combination of a 3+1 spacetime ontology and presentism. As Sections 4.1 and 4.2 will show, whichever interpretation of spacetime one endorses, significant concerns arise regarding the viability of Christian theism. Can salvation itself be saved?

4.1 Personal Salvation as a Transformation in Time

The first problem spacetime poses for salvation is that personal salvation requires a temporal transformation. This problem is specifically raised if a four-dimensional interpretation of spacetime is true – in other words, it arises only in the block universe that accompanies a B-theory or C-theory of time. The problem is as follows: salvation requires an objective change from fallenness to redemption that, at the very least, begins to occur within the spatio-temporal lifetime of the fallen individual. Within the block universe's static temporal ontology, where time does not pass and nothing comes into or goes out of existence, objective change of the kind required by many readings of the Christian doctrine of salvation is highly problematised. Yet a personal transformation seems integral to the Christian salvation-redemption narrative. If physics and metaphysics, particularly their descriptions of spacetime, seem to rule out the possibility of objective, robust change, then the Christian faces an acute problem. So, the question arises, how can we understand a personal salvation transformation in the block universe?

4.1.1 The Problem

Before answering this question, I will set out the problem in a little more detail. Christianity involves commitment to some form of personal salvation. Salvation is a broad and multifaceted concept, and reflection on the human quest for salvation has an extremely rich history. A common thread that runs throughout all formulations is that salvation is the search for authentic life. It involves *change* from a prior state in which an individual or group is unfulfilled or falling short personally or relationally, to a state of authenticity, fulfilment, and rich relationality (with other people, with the natural world, or with the divine). This change is typically understood to mean that the individual's sins are *gone* (forgiven, washed away) and the individual has entered a *new* mode of being in which they are wholly and objectively reconciled to God. We see such claims in Scripture: 'if we confess our sins, he is faithful and just to forgive us our sins and to cleanse us from all unrighteousness' (1 John 1:9); 'if anyone is in Christ, he is a new creation. The old has passed away; behold, the new has come' (2 Corinthians 5:7). As Richard Holland writes, 'These passages and others indicate a finality: a transformation achieved through the work of Christ that brings about a new standing before God (Holland 2012: 183–4).

Salvation is always salvation *from* something; it assumes both humanity and the world are distorted, self-destructive, and failing to reach our true potential. Typically, how one conceptualises salvation depends upon one's understanding of the human predicament in the cultural context in which salvation occurs. Paul Fiddes argues that the task of theology is locating where the 'mystery in our midst' is to be found (Fiddes 1989: 5). For Christians, salvation or atonement depends upon a particular moment in time and space at which point Jesus of Nazareth was crucified on a cross. This event is believed to be the centre point in human history, dividing the fallen old creation from the eschatological promise of a new creation made possible by Jesus' resurrection.

Fiddes identifies three core features of the human predicament which occur in all doctrines of atonement. The first is a sense of alienation/ estrangement. This can be understood as a loss of contact with one's social fabric, distance from the divine, or distance from oneself. Such themes are culturally ubiquitous, from Hegelian philosophy to Shakespeare's sonnets. The second is a failure to fulfil potential, both our individual potential and the potential of our species. As Jean-Paul Sartre puts it, we have an 'unhappy consciousness' that reaches out to what we always lack (Sartre and Barnes 1957: 90). The third feature, sin, is specifically Christian. Ian McFarland writes that 'the semantic range of the term "sin" includes not only particular *acts* that contravene God's will, but also the congenital *state* of opposition to God that subsists apart from and prior to any specific actions a person performs' (McFarland 2007: 141).

Scripture identifies the root of sin as Adam and Eve's first disobedience, the consequences of which are passed down throughout human history (Genesis 2–3). Christian doctrine teaches that sin permeates the very nature of humanity and is manifested in every act in which a person turns away from God. This picture of sin as a quasi-personal power largely stems from the Pauline literature in which it was initially developed. It can be characterised as unbelief, a failure to trust in the Christian message and the life it recommends, or a rejection of God in favour of earthly things. Sin creates the conditions of fallenness, that from which the Christian hopes to be saved. It has both individual and relational components. Much has been written on sin, and unfortunately the concept's rich theological history is not within the scope of the present work. In the broadest terms, sin is that from which individuals are saved.

Whilst one's understanding of the finer details of salvation may vary in accordance with one's specific theological predilections, all are committed to some form of personal transformation. Whether the individual attains salvation in this lifetime or the next, this process is believed to at least begin during individuals' finite, spatio-temporal, existence. Indeed, many view it as the entire purpose of this finite, spatio-temporal, existence. Thus, a temporal metaphysic that is able to accommodate objective change is required. In the block universe, however, every event that occurs (within spacetime) always tenselessly exists. The Moon landing, for example, has always been within the block universe. If you are a B-theorist, all events preceding 20 July 1969 have always been in a *before than* relation with it, and all events after 20 July 1969 have always been in an *after than* relation to it. Neither the event nor its relations with other events can change.

If you are a C-theorist, the events in the block universe are only ordered by relations of temporal betweenness – the Moon landing, for example, is *between* the coronation of Queen Elizabeth and her death. It cannot change its place in the fixed temporal series of which it is part. Additionally, within the block universe no spacetime slice, frontier, or moment is ontologically privileged. In other words, there is no objective *now* which changes with the passage of time. Because of this, McTaggart argued that the B-theory cannot accommodate change (McTaggart 1908: 459). Although debate continues concerning the success of his argument, I argue that it poses a problem for many traditional formulations of the doctrine of salvation. Salvation requires both that sin be washed away and that the sinner can objectively transform *from* a fallen state *to* a new, redeemed state.

The A-theory's objective temporal dynamism easily allows the type of objective and ontological change required by many formulations of the doctrine of salvation. Absolute, flowing time gives rise to the mind-independent *coming into being* of new entities, events, and properties, accommodating what I will call *robust change* with ease. For robust change to take place, it must be the case that one and the same entity has gone from objectively possessing some property or properties at time t, to possessing some incompatible property or properties at time t'. For example, an insect has undergone a robust change if it is a caterpillar at t and a butterfly at t'; a person has undergone a robust change if they have a luscious head of hair at t and are bald at t'. Importantly when this is applied to salvation, the prior state must be objectively gone (otherwise the whole individual, namely the entire four-dimensional extension, has not been cleansed of sin and is not completely saved). Robust change thus defined requires genuine *newness* of a kind that does not appear to be compatible with the metaphysics of the block universe. This type of change is particularly important for salvation for two reasons: (1) salvific change is generally understood to be both total and objective and (2) salvation is the result of Christ entering reality at a certain historical moment to be present in creation in a way that he was not before. Both of these seem to require robust change – the saved person comes to possess new soteriological properties, and Christ brought something fundamentally new into the cosmos.

Robin Le Poidevin explores a variant of this problem, which he puts thus:

'(1) The Atonement resulted from a final, once-for-all sacrifice for our sins.

(2) For the Atonement to have been final in this sense, our unredeemed state must be objectively past.

(3) The B-theory denies that anything is objectively past. Therefore:

(4) Our understanding of the significance of the Atonement requires a rejection of the B-theory.' (Le Poidevin 2016: 186)

On this formulation of the problem, salvation faces problems on a B-theory as the prior, fallen state cannot be said to be objectively past. Le Poidevin develops his argument further, writing:

> On the B-theory, there is no such ontological asymmetry between past and future... With no passage of time, there is no scope for any change in what is real. For 'real' is not similarly perspectival. On this theory, then, the Atonement, if real at any time, is real with respect to all time: its reality does not change over time. It seems that we are left with a choice between two uncongenial possibilities: (i) since the Atonement is at all times part of reality, and since the Atonement is sufficient for restoring our relationship with God for all time, then at no time is God unreconciled to humanity; (ii) since the sin that broke our relationship with God is at all times part of reality, and since that sin separates us from God, then at no time are we reconciled to God... Either way, there is no change from fallen to redeemed state for man.
>
> (Le Poidevin 2016: 189–90)

If a state exists in the B-theory, it exists *simpliciter*, neither coming into nor going out of existence. But salvation requires an objective, ontological change between states which leaves sin objectively in the past, and brings a *new* relationship with the divine. Ultimately, Le Poidevin appeals to asymmetrical causal relations to argue that the B-theorist can say the prior fallen states are in *their* past and are causally prior to Christ's atoning act. By virtue of the sinful parts being causally antecedent to the saved parts, we can properly say that the individual has undergone a progressive soteriological transformation. It remains to be seen whether this type of response is enough to get us the robust change attested to in Scripture.

Whether or not robust change is possible seems to depend upon which temporal metaphysic accurately captures reality. On an A-theory, if some entity e is x at time t and y at time t', then when time objectively passes from t to t', e has objectively changed from x to y. Thus, the A-theory contains the appropriate metaphysical architecture within which robust change can take place. In the block universe, however, if entity e is x at time t and y at time t', then there is no objective way to say whether e is x or y. Both t and t' are equally, tenselessly, real. Using the metaphysics of spacetime, at least, there is no way to say which one *e* actually is. It is not enough to index the properties to times and then say that the *later* properties supersede the *earlier* properties, as this still does not give either time (and its corresponding property) ontological priority. *E* is both *x* and *y*, just at different (equally real) times. This applies to individuals as well. If a person, let's call them Jack, is fallen at time *t* and saved at time *t′*, then in the block universe there is no way to say whether Jack is objectively fallen or saved – they are both fallen and saved at different points in their four-dimensional extension, and these points have equal ontological status. Therefore, the block universe interpretation of spacetime raises a serious problem for the Christian insofar as their doctrine of salvation requires a robust change from being fallen to being saved.

This stems, in part, from how we understand personal identity in the block universe. One option is known as perdurantism, in which persons are four-dimensional extensions comprising temporal parts. On this view, your entire self is never present at any moment of your life – you have temporal parts that are eating lunch today, temporal parts that do not yet know what you will eat for lunch today, and temporal parts that have forgotten what you ate for lunch today. All these parts are equally (though not the entirety of) you.

If both an A-theory and perdurantism are correct, then prior temporal parts disappear into the non-existent past as new ones come into being. Ben Page has suggested that this might be a way to conceive of an ontological transformation (specifically, one in which a believer becomes a 'new creation' *a la* Paul's proclamation in 2 Corinthians 5:17). In this model, the individual is ontologically transformed through the replacement of some of their temporal parts from sinful parts to saved parts. The sinful parts have disappeared, and so the individual is truly transformed (Page 2018: 534).

If a B-theory and perdurantism are correct, however, then all your temporal parts eternally exist. You are a four-dimensional 'worm' that is extended across all the events in your spatio-temporal lifetime. The relevance of this for personal salvation is as follows: your four-dimensional ontology does not change. If you have fallen temporal parts in the block universe (which presumably Christians want to say is the case for everyone), then you always have fallen parts. These cannot be truly left behind, even if you do possess subsequent saved temporal parts. Whilst they may *seem* left behind from the perspective of your later parts, this is only perspectival. Your four-dimensional ontology cannot change, and so your fallen parts remain as much a part of you as any other parts. This seems to lead to the striking conclusion that sinners cannot really change.

So, we have reached the crux of the issue: the Christian doctrine of salvation appears to require that individuals undergo, or at least begin to undergo, an objective, ontological, change in this lifetime. Yet in the block universe, nothing new comes into being and nothing old fades away. An individual's sinful, fallen temporal parts exist for as long as the block universe does, sharing an equal ontological status to any subsequent, saved parts. Thus, nothing within our best understanding of spacetime can metaphysically substantiate the theist's claim that fallen individuals can undergo an objective salvation transformation. In the block universe, the soteriological requirement that sinners can change is deeply problematised. In the next section I will sketch out my own solution to this problem, building on arguments I have made elsewhere (Qureshi-Hurst and Pearson 2020; Qureshi-Hurst 2022).

4.1.2 A Solution

One of the ways this problem can be solved, I will argue, is to reconceptualise what is involved in a soteriological transformation. If we think of the transformation an individual begins to undergo in their lifetime not as *objective* and *ontological* change, but instead *subjective* and *phenomenological* change, then the beginnings of a solution emerges. In other words, the problem of salvation in the block universe can begin to be overcome by proposing that salvation takes place via an alternative type of change which I call *mind-dependent salvific becoming*.

Essentially, I will argue that as the mind constructs passage phenomenology (i.e. the phenomenal experience of the passage of time) out of ordered events in the block universe, so too can the mind construct a soteriological transformation. The saved individual goes through a subjective, psychological, qualitative change, which for them constitutes, corresponds to, and provide evidence of personal salvation. This is best articulated in dialogue with the philosophy of temporal experience, as important advances have been made here that provide the conceptual building blocks out of which a partial solution to the problem of salvation and spacetime can be built (see Section 1.3).

In recent years, interest in the nature of temporal experience has grown. Many (though, interestingly, not all) agree that certain features of our experience seem to us to be *as of* temporal passage (the *as of* caveat is neutral about whether this experience is veridical). As previously noted, this is not a problem for the A-theorist as they endorse the reality of temporal passage, and thus no issue in relating incongruent temporal experience and temporal theory arises (Craig 2000: 133). The B-theorist and C-theorist, however, are called to provide an explanation of passage phenomenology that does not depend on the existence of dynamic time. Several such proposals have been offered (see Section 1.3 for a brief summary of some key candidates). Adolf Grünbaum supplied one such explanation, which provides conceptual architecture within which a solution to the problem at hand can be constructed.

Grünbaum locates the source of temporal experience in the mind's subjective interpretation of the world, as opposed to some ontological feature of mind-independent reality. Subsequent scholarship has built upon Grünbaum's proposal, incorporating data from experimental psychology and cognitive science. One such example is the aforementioned argument from Robin Le Poidevin (Section 1.3) which constitutes, in Ian Phillips' view, a 'memory theory of succession' (Phillips 2009: 443). Le Poidevin's central thesis is that A-properties are projected onto the world in response to certain features of experience. Another example is Laurie Paul, also discussed in Section 1.3, who compares motion pictures generated from many still frames and our temporal experience, which she argues is generated by our brains through experiencing cognitive inputs from a series of static events and B-facts. Each of these creates an 'illusion of animation'. As Deng summarises: 'in a nutshell, the recommendation is: if you are a B-theorist, think of life as a whole as a kind of film' (Deng 2013: 375).

There are other B-theoretic proposals besides these, which unfortunately fall outside the scope of this work. My focus will be on the so-called Illusionism of Grünbaum, although one can imagine how one might flesh out *mind-dependent salvific becoming* using tools from other B-theoretic Illusionists. Grünbaum notes that the respect with which events are deemed to change is intimately connected to passage (Grünbaum 1971: 195). The experience of successive present moments is an essential feature of passage, and as such his account of temporal experience hinges on the concept of *presentness* or *nowness*. More specifically, Grünbaum centres his account of becoming on the status of the present as a property of events which is encountered in perceptual awareness.

Grünbaum, along with several philosophers since, compares temporal properties like nowness with sensory properties like colour. These comparisons ground his use of *mind-dependence* which is so central to his analysis of temporal experience. Time, much like colour, is apparent to the conscious subject as a result of certain external stimuli from which the mind constructs powerful but subjective meaning. Colour is a secondary quality that emerges out of our sensory faculties perceiving various wavelengths of light which objects absorb and reflect. Similarly, Grünbaum argues that the mind constructs temporal passage out of the static events of the block universe. Thus, temporal experience does not have representational content; it is, instead, mind-dependent.

Following with this, Grünbaum denies that *presentness* exists mind-independently. What is necessary instead to qualify some event e as being present at time t is at least one conscious, mind-possessing being (i.e. a person) M being conceptually aware either of experiencing e or of experiencing some other event that is simultaneous with *e* in *M*'s reference frame (Grünbaum 1971: 206). By experiencing successive subjectively defined presents, dynamic temporal experience is generated. In other words, passage phenomenology is subjectively generated by the minds of conscious beings who experience successive *now* moments which are perceptually immediate, and that the mind takes to be present. Through the attribution of the adverbial property *now*, and the experience of successive nows, the mind constructs becoming, and we experience time as if it passes.

This can be applied to an individual's experience of a salvation transformation. On this view, conscious awareness plays a highly important role in phenomenologically substantiating the type of change required to transform an individual's life from a state of fallenness to a state of salvation. Essentially, individuals can choose to instantiate actions which lead to an authentic, soteriologically directed, life, and then experience a transformation from fallenness to (or towards) salvation. Though this will always have been in one's future, and so in that sense it is not radically new or undetermined, one's future salvation comes into one's perceptual awareness as something apparently new. In other words, one's soteriological state is subjectively and phenomenologically new, despite not being the result of anything new in an objective or ontological sense.

Mind-dependent becoming is, I argue, a helpful way of understanding salvation in the block universe, but it remains to address what kind of change this involves. C. D. Broad's assessment of McTaggart in *An Examination of McTaggart's Philosophy* introduces a useful concept for our purposes: qualitative change. Broad defines qualitative change as a mode of change involving a subject acquiring qualities that they did not possess previously. To develop his point, Broad distinguishes between events which do not change and *things* which do (Broad 1938: 317). Things – persisting entities – can possess different properties at different times and as such are susceptible to qualitative change.

Qualitative change has occurred when an individual possesses different properties at different temporal points in their four-dimensional extension. The block universe interpretation of spacetime easily accommodates this type of change – a subject's various temporal parts can possess different properties without having to invoke the reality of tense to say which set of properties that subject possesses *now*. I will explore what this looks like through an analogy with a metal poker. Imagine a poker half in a fire such that it is heated at one end. This end it is white hot, whilst the other end is dark silver and much cooler. In the middle portions the poker ranges from yellow to orange, cherry red to a deep burgundy in accordance with its proximity to the flames. One could not reasonably ask which single colour or temperature the poker is objectively, for it is all of them at different points. If your line of sight was moving up the poker, you would subjectively experience a qualitative change in its colour and temperature. But this change is a product of your perception, not evidence that the whole object has undergone an objective change.

I want to suggest that the hot poker is analogous to a four-dimensional extension of the self, insofar as that self possesses different properties at different parts of their extension. Within the block universe, there is no observer-independent way to say which property you possess objectively, or which property you possess *now* (where now is understood as absolute and universal). Rather, you possess all these properties at different spatio-temporal locations in the four-dimensional extension of yourself. As such, I argue that the only way to conceptualise personal salvation (understood as a transformation in time) is subjectively.

Mind-dependent becoming offers an explanation for our experience of passage whereby the conscious mind constructs passage phenomenology out of the successive experience of static events. Applying this to salvation, an individual in the block universe can undergo a qualitative, phenomenological, change from fallen to saved by possessing the properties associated with each soteriological state at different times. As they experience these properties successively, they experience this *as* robust change. This is analogous to the experience of time as robustly passing, despite neither robust change nor robust passage being real (i.e. mind-independent or objective). Thus, our experience of such change is illusory in the same way our experience of passage is illusory.

Nevertheless, this does not mean that the salvation itself is illusory. On the contrary, it is still possible for the saved individual to objectively possess the property of being fallen at certain spatio-temporal locations and objectively possess the property of being saved at other spatio-temporal locations. The experience of robustly changing between these two states is illusory insofar as neither is a genuinely new state which was not already present in the block universe or the four-dimensional extension of an individual's being. Yet just as the events in the block universe are real and ground an (illusory) phenomenology of robust passage, so too are the properties of being fallen and being saved objectively real. So, whilst the B-theory cannot accommodate a robust soteriological change, and the sinful parts can neither cease to exist nor have inferior ontological status, some form of soteriological change is possible.

There are two alternative and equally viable interpretations of what this might look like. One might imagine a sudden, Damascene conversion – a stark and immediate change from one mode of being to another. On the other hand, one might understand this as a more gradual transformation from fallenness to reconciliation, with many in-between stages. This reflects the type of transformation an individual may undergo over several months or years, as they gradually allow themselves to be grasped by the saving power of the Spirit and experience the renewed relationality with the divine that follows. Nevertheless, on both views it remains the case that your sinful past parts are not gone. They may seem gone from your later temporal parts' perspective, but from a God's eye perspective, those sinful parts remain. Perhaps this reveals the need for eschatological considerations to enter the conversation. Perhaps it is only once this world is no more that the soteriological process can reach ultimate fulfilment, and the total washing away of sin becomes complete.

In this section I have argued that the block universe model of spacetime poses a genuine threat to the possibility of personal salvation insofar as it is hostile to robust change. I have offered a solution to this problem that draws on insights from the philosophy of temporal experience, particularly the work of Adolf Grünbaum. Through experiencing your life events successively, individuals experience qualitative change. I argue that this can, and actually should, be applied to salvation. The result is mind-dependent salvific becoming, a subjective understanding of salvation that can nonetheless hold deep soteriological significance for the saved individual. Though this may be a weaker form of soteriological change than some may like, I argue that it is the best possible model of personal salvation that can occur within the block universe. Therefore, it makes a valuable contribution to the search for a solution to the problem of spacetime and personal salvation.

4.2 Eschatological Transformation and the End of the Universe

The previous problem posed for salvation by spacetime arose in a specifically B and C-theoretic context, namely the block universe or four-dimensional model of spacetime. The problem under consideration in this section is one of *eschatology* and is specifically raised if presentism, by far the most widely endorsed A-theory, is true. Presentism involves commitment to a 3+1 spacetime ontology, whereby three-dimensional space and one-dimensional time remain separate. As opposed to a four-dimensional spacetime ontology in which space and time form a single fabric, 3+1 spacetime contains slices of absolute space (hypersurfaces) strung together by absolute time.

On presentism, when present spacelike hypersurfaces become past, they cease to exist. This raises serious concerns for the plausibility of bodily resurrection. As time passes and the body decays, all spacelike hypersurfaces that contain the decaying body vanish into non-existence until nothing is left. No body exists to recover, and bodily resurrection (that involves the *exact same body*) becomes difficult to accommodate. Also problematised is the idea that this physical creation will be transformed into a new creation at the end-times. This is especially the case if presentism is combined with cosmological predictions of the end of the universe, a turn of events that would leave the cosmos and its contents decayed or destroyed. In this section, I explore the problems that emerge from a presentist 3+1 spacetime ontology along with some of the solutions that have been proposed.

Eschatology is understood here as the study of final things, namely: death, judgement, heaven, hell, and the end of the universe. In the following, I will sketch out, in extremely broad brushstrokes, how Christian theology has traditionally understood this. Christianity bears witness to a creator God who brought the universe into being for a purpose. That purpose is believed to be, in part, for the universe and (maybe a select few, maybe all) its inhabitants to enter into a loving, covenantal, relationship with God. In order to realise this purpose, God decrees that humanity must live first in the created physical universe which is plagued by sin and fallenness. These are caused and characterised differently depending on one's theological predilections. In this earthly lifetime humans are estranged from God, but because of the soteriological work of Jesus Christ and the ongoing presence of the Spirit, individuals are able to exercise the freedom to come to God and begin to undergo a process of personal salvation (see Section 4.1). Then, they die.

At the end-times, (maybe a select few, maybe all) persons are raised from the dead and redeemed, reaching the eschatological goal of creation by being transformed into a 'new creation' characterised by eternal life and unity with God. This resurrection is believed to echo Christ's resurrection insofar as it involves your physical body and not just your immaterial soul. Your body will 'be raised imperishable, and . . . will be changed' (1 Corinthians 15:52). Whilst the raised body will exhibit important material differences from the body you inhabit at this present moment, it must nonetheless be continuous with that body in certain key respects.

The same is believed to be the case for the rest of creation. Romans 8:18–30, for example, speaks of the groaning of creation and the promise of eschatological redemption for the entire physical universe. Parallels are drawn in these verses between the eschatological promise of bodily resurrection and the redemption of all the created order. In the words of John Polkinghorne, 'the resurrection of Jesus is the seminal event from which the whole of God's new creation has already begun to grow' (Polkinghorne 2002: 113). This applies to humanity and the universe equally. The Christian is therefore committed to the claim that the universe itself will be redeemed and will become a new creation. In summary, eschatology traditionally requires (1) that physical creation persists in such a way that it can be transformed into a new creation, and (2) that the physical bodies of human beings can be raised to spend eternity with God. Though this is a very brief and broad description of a complex set of doctrinal claims, it captures the key ideas relevant to the problem at hand.

It is widely agreed that eschatology is an essential component of the Christian worldview. Indeed, twentieth-century theologian Karl Barth went so far as to say that 'Christianity that is not entirely and altogether eschatology has entirely and altogether nothing to do with Christ' (Barth 1933: 314). Recent scholarship has seen an increase in explorations of the relationship between eschatology and the physical sciences, as both concern the nature (and the future) of the world. David Wilkinson writes, for example, that systematic theologians are primarily concerned with doing eschatology 'in the real world', helping to keep theo-logical thinking fresh and relevant for each new generation. We also see this in Paul Tillich's method of correlation which seeks to give age-old theological answers to cutting-edge cultural questions (Tillich 1947). Tillich is certainly not alone in favouring this kind of approach. There is an increasing appetite for eschatology to enter into dialogue with both science and philosophy. Within 'science and religion', a significant amount of attention has been given to whether contemporary physics, especially cosmology, can provide theologic-ally useful insights as to what the eschatological culmination of the universe might look like.

Contemporary cosmology is founded upon Einstein's General Theory of Relativity. As we have seen, GR describes the behaviour of massive objects and their interactions with spacetime (a.k.a. the gravitational field). Coupling GR's equations with observational data on distant stars and galaxies, including Hubble's observation of galactic red-shift, shows that the universe is expanding. From this, physicists can predict how the universe will evolve over time, and their best cosmological predictions suggest that the universe will come to an end. There are various candidate possibilities for what the end of the universe will look like, but the two primary contenders are known colloquially as *freeze* and *fry*.

The former, *freeze*, refers to the heat-death of the universe. Whether *freeze* is a viable option will depend on the value of the cosmological constant (Λ), namely the energy density of the vacuum of space. The cosmological constant acts as a counterbalance to gravity, thus its value determines the relative strength of gravity and will have a significant impact on the fate of the cosmos. If Λ turns out to be stronger than a certain critical value, then the energy density of space will prevent gravity from mitigating the expansive consequences of the Big Bang. This means that the universe will continue to expand and cool for the rest of time. Over many billions of years, galaxies will vanish over the horizon, stars will burn out, atoms will decay, and the universe will reach maximum entropy in a soup of black holes and radiation whose temperature tends toward absolute zero. This universe would be totally dark, extremely cold, and no life of any kind could hope to survive.

The latter, *fry*, sometimes also called the Big Crunch, is for all practical purposes the reverse of the Big Bang. If Λ is weaker than a certain critical value, then gravity will eventually halt the universe's expansion and cause it to begin collapsing back in on itself. If this occurs, then stars, planets, and galaxies will rush toward each other, the skies viewed from planets will shine with the brightness of a thousand suns, and eventually everything will implode into an extremely hot, infinitely dense, and definitely uninhabitable, singularity. Though the physics is rather more complicated than this brief description, the salient point is that the universe looks set to end in either a *freeze* or a *fry* scenario.

Though physicists cannot be certain about which of these will occur, recent findings indicate that the universe's expansion is accelerating, perhaps due to a higher value of Λ than previously expected. If correct, this swings the balance of probability in favour of *freeze*. Although we do not yet know which of these scenarios will happen, we do know that each entails the end of our universe and the destruction or decay of its contents. As John Polkinghorne writes: 'science presents us with the picture of a universe that, despite its present fruitfulness, will eventually end in the futility of cosmic collapse or decay' (Polkinghorne 2002: xviii). Whatever happens, human beings will not survive indefinitely.

This raises a specific set of challenges for certain understandings of Christian eschatology. Robert John Russell puts the problem thus:

> For those who defend the bodily resurrection . . . the challenge is obvious and severe: if the predictions of contemporary scientific cosmology come to pass ('freeze' or 'fry') then it would seem that the universe will never be transformed into a new creation, that there will never be a general resurrection, and this, in turn, means that Christ has not been raised from the dead, and our hope for resurrection and eternal life is in vain. (Russell 2002b: 267)

Importantly, this catastrophic conclusion emerges only when combined with presentism. If presentism is true, then the entirety of creation will vanish forever when the universe ends, destroyed as it fades into the not-real past. Given this, the eschatological hope of redeeming physical creation by transforming it into something new (whilst retaining continuity with the old) seems wholly unfounded.

The block universe does not face the same issues. This can be explained through considering the block universe's resemblance to a novel. If the universe is to end, then the proponent of the block universe need only consider this ending the final page in the universe's story. All other pages still exist, meaning human beings and physical creation are out there somewhere in the block universe even if that universe has a finite ending; a last page after which the universal story is over. A novel, and every page within it, does not vanish out of existence once the final page has been read. Similarly, each time-slice of the universe still exists in the block universe and is available for resurrection or redemption if God so chooses. On presentism, however, the scientific promise of the end of the universe entails the total destruction or degradation of the universe and everything it has ever contained. Nothing will endure that can be saved, redeemed, or transformed.

The contemporary context within which real-world eschatology must be articulated includes the aforementioned scientific predictions of the end of the universe and the destruction or degradation of its contents. It is increasingly being acknowledged that bringing modern science into dialogue with scripture generates important insights for how to understand eschatology. So, both bodily resurrection and the possibility of a new creation are utterly integral to the biblical witness, and therefore to Christianity as a whole. But are these still scientifically credible options?

4.2.1 Bodily Resurrection

Without a block universe metaphysic, it is unclear how bodily resurrection can be compatible with the end of the universe. As Russell remarks, 'the physical sciences, including cosmology, raise tremendous, perhaps insurmountable, challenges to the intelligibility of "bodily resurrection"' (Russell 2002b: 273). Whilst it is the case that many branches of science raise potential problems for bodily resurrection, the focus here will be on the concerns raised by contemporary cosmology, particularly regarding the rather bleak ultimate fate of our spatio-temporal universe. Simply put, in the block universe all temporal parts of all individual persons (and universe stages) coexist and can be 'retrieved' by God at any time. On presentism, however, each time-slice vanishes irretrievably into the unreal past when it ceases to be present. Thus, the end of the universe and the destruction and degradation of its contents means that physical resurrection seems nigh on impossible. There is simply nothing left to be resurrected.

Whilst an omnipotent God could easily re-create individuals anew in the Kingdom of Heaven, this is not what is claimed in scripture. It is hard to see how that could be a *resurrection* of persons, as opposed to a *recreation* of persons. Scripture promises that individual persons will be raised, enter the Kingdom of Heaven, and live out eternity in glory with God. There must be some level of continuity between the person who died and the person who is raised again in order to be consistent with that claim. Nor, many believe, could God simply save an immaterial soul and leave the physical body to decay and, ultimately, disappear.

John Polkinghorne develops the latter claim, arguing that human beings are much more like animated bodies than incarnate souls. We see this in the evolutionary story, biblical witness, and in more recent work on embodied cognition. Thus, the Christian cannot fall back on a substance dualist, 'ghost in the machine', view of the relation between mind and body. In a way, this is an unfortunate consequence for the Christian. They must face head-on the far thornier problem of bodily resurrection, and cannot simply claim that the survival of an immaterial soul is sufficient to fulfil scripture's eschatological promises. The physical body must be raised and redeemed for the promises of the future to come to pass.

Polkinghorne argues that the solution lies in thinking of the soul not as a ghost in the machine, but instead as a pattern of information, which he describes as Aquinas with a modern twist. He writes: 'amid its evolving change, each individual soul carries specific elements of its patterning which are the signature of its own abiding and unique personal identity. (A mathematician would say that there were invariant characters, preserved in the course of unfolding transformation.)' (Polkinghorne 2002: 107). Polkinghorne affirms that death is real death – the soul is encoded in the body and so dies with bodily decay – but can be preserved in divine memory (like a shadow) and could be reembodied by an omnipotent God. God preserves the soul (thus understood) and therein lies eternal life. This would constitute a physical resurrection, he argues, not simply the eternal endurance of an immortal soul. Ultimately, then, he is optimistic about the possibility of resurrection in the face of *freeze* or *fry* scenarios.

David Wilkinson, too, confronts this problem, grounding much of his discussion of resurrection in the biblical narratives. In 1 Corinthians Paul explores bodily resurrection through the metaphor of a seed which is planted in the ground and then given by God a body into which it grows. Similarly, for people, 'the body that is sown is perishable, it is raised imperishable; it is sown in dishonour, it is raised in glory; it is sown in weakness, it is raised in power; it is sown a natural body, it is raised a spiritual body' (1 Corinthians 15:42–44). One thing is certain – Paul believed that resurrection entails a fundamental change in the raised person. Such change must be different from the ordinary changes we seem to undergo all the time, that is, when we continuously exchange atoms with the universe around us, when our cells undergo renewal, and when our bodies age. This change must even be understood as importantly different from the kind of personal soteriological transformation that an individual begins to undergo in their lifetime (as explored in Section 4.1).

There remains much debate about the precise meaning of this passage, especially the extent to which Paul wishes to emphasise continuity between the 'sewn' sinful body and the raised glorious body, and how much he understood the raised body as discontinuous, thereby utterly different in kind, from the original sinful body. Regarding discontinuity, Wilkinson discusses Anthony Thiselton's claim that personhood is fundamentally dynamic. According to Thiselton we are constantly changing, including the fact that we begin to die from remarkably early on in life (somewhere around age twenty-five). Thiselton takes this sort of idea and applies it to the concept of resurrection, arguing that it is better understood as being a reversal of decay or a purposeful flourishing, like the curing of a wasting disease. On this type of view, the destruction of the physical universe does little to disrupt the eschatological process, as that decay is able to be reversed or regenerated. It is not the exact same physical *stuff* that is resurrected so much as the *identity*.

Can redemption really occur without the physical body? On the one hand, human beings are more than machines made of meat. We exist in a network of relationships, structure our lives in accordance with narratives that give us meaning and purpose, and we cannot truly understand ourselves in isolationist terms. If the Kingdom of Heaven is to reflect that, then surely it must also include our hopes, passions, relationships, communities, and all the other component parts that make up our complex and evolving identities. One could imagine a scenario in which these components are preserved whilst the body is not. The body does not seem to be as integral as we might imagine when considering creation (and our place within it) holistically.

Nevertheless, it may turn out that our sense of self, even in the above respects, is inescapable physical. Recent work on embodied cognition indicates that we are fundamentally physical beings whose selfhood is bound-up with our bodies in such a way that an immaterial mind would not be a continuation of the self at all (Shapiro 2012). Indeed, according to embodied cognition theorists, there cannot even be a mind without a body. In an extended exploration of the nature of human rationality, Alister McGrath writes on similar themes:

> Human thinkers are embodied, existing in a complex relationship with their physical and social environment, involving both top-down and bottom-up interactions which make it impossible to treat cognitive functioning in a culturally or socially detached manner. The human mind creates culture, which in turn interacts with the manner in which that mind functions, thus creating a complex layered framework of interaction and feedback. (McGrath 2019)

This is indicative of an emerging consensus that emphasises the importance of embodiment, culture, and contextuality in human cognition and human identity more widely. Embodied cognition recognises that we cannot unambiguously draw a clear distinction between mind and body, nor between person and world. As Rebekah Wallace writes, 'Embodied Cognition (EC) [is] beginning to break down [the] dualism that leads to a view of the world as constituted primarily by parts. EC sees the mind and its cognitive processes not as a static, information-processing entity, but as an emergent property of the dynamic interplay of body and world' (Wallace 2022). In light of work in embodied cognition, then, individuals are increasingly understood as fundamentally and irreducibly situated in wider contexts of cultural, intellectual, and spiritual meaning. Our minds, and therefore (arguably) our identities, cannot exist apart from the physical bodies that inhabit these contexts.

Our bodies are markers of our individual identities and, in many ways, form the basis of our cultural and sub-cultural networks of relationships. This is true in the relatively superficial contexts of self-expression and subculture adherence through clothing, hair-dye, and makeup, and in deeper and more authentic contexts of ethnic and cultural expressions of selfhood that form the basis of communities (both natural characteristics like skin colour and culturally significant body modification including religious tattooing play a part in this). In numerous ways that vary in how deeply they relate to our core sense of self, physical embodiment is a highly significant component of human identity. So the question remains, what actually becomes of this physical stuff out of which the body is made? And can we truly exist (in temporal creation or eternity) without it? Here, the problem under consideration comes to a head. How can that which is resurrected have physical continuity with the original body if the body, along with the entire universe, is destroyed in a *freeze* or *fry* scenario?

Perhaps the answer lies in the gospel accounts of the resurrection, as the resurrection of Jesus is typically held to be the 'first fruits' of our eschatological future. The New Testament bears witness to the resurrection of Jesus, God-the-Son, and implies that this is a sign of what is to come for believers. However, as David Wilkinson points out, whilst the first fruits indicate that the harvest is coming, they are different to the harvest in certain key respects. For one, Jesus' body was raised very soon after his death. Yet our bodies will have undergone significant, perhaps total, decay in the time that elapses between death and possible resurrection. Wilkinson points to the fact that Jesus did, however, lay in the tomb for three days before rising again, and did not just immediately reanimate. This reveals, he argues, the importance of *time* in the transformation that brings (or foreshadows the bringing of) the new creation. If Jesus rose again within and over the course of time, so too should we expect the corresponding transformation of creation to occur within and over the course of time (Wilkinson 2010: 94).

The gospels emphasise the bodily continuity of the risen Jesus – he is recognised (John 20:19–20), he can be touched (Matthew 28:9), and he bears the unmistakable marks of his crucifixion (Luke 24:39). In these passages, it is clear that Jesus' actual body rose again, and that physical continuity is therefore essential. Thus, the original body must not be utterly abandoned if the resurrection of believers is to echo the resurrection of Christ. Despite this, there are also important discontinuities – Jesus appears to have new physical properties that allow him to appear in locked rooms (John 20:19–20) and that cause some to doubt whether it is really him (Luke 24:37). Wilkinson acknowledges that the gospel accounts of the resurrection are 'untidy', out of which a single, clear, picture of resurrection emerges hazily if it emerges at all (Wilkinson 2010: 101–2).

Wilkinson eventually lands upon the claim that the continuity between the fallen earthly body and the raised body is founded upon the transformative power of God: 'the key to resurrection and new creation is not the importance of the material but the action of the creator God' (Wilkinson 2010: 100). Physical creation contains various kinds of matter, substance, and form, all of which, on the Christian worldview, are dependent wholly on God the creator. So, too, with the new body in the new creation. The resurrection, on Wilkinson's view, must be thought of as a divinely ordained transformation from decay to purposeful flourishing. Ultimately, however, bodily resurrection must not be thought of in self-centred, individualistic terms. Nor should we focus too closely on the kind of substance out of which the new body will be composed. Instead, resurrection must be understood within a much broader cosmological context. In other words, when discussing bodily resurrection, one cannot focus on the body *alone*. Resurrection occurs only within the framework of a new creation. It is to this new creation that we now turn.

4.2.2 New Creation

Along with bodily resurrection, Christian scripture also attests to the eschatological promise of a new creation. This new creation must be discontinuous with the old creation insofar as it is genuinely new, possessing fresh soteriological and eschatological properties that render it transformed. Nevertheless, one must not view the new creation as 'a second attempt by God to do what he had tried first to do in the old creation', the new creation is instead held to be 'a divine redemption of the old' (Polkinghorne 1994: 167). In other words, it must still be *creation*, despite its newness. The empty tomb demonstrates that the substance of this creation, as well as the flesh and bones of human beings, matters to God. As Wilkinson writes, 'the new creation is a transformation, renewal or purification of the present creation rather than a total annihilation and beginning again' (Wilkinson 2010: 86). So, how can the Christian reconcile the end of the universe with the promise that physical creation will be redeemed eschatologically?

Wilkinson's own view draws on the literature on God, time, and eternity (Section 3). First, he argues that God is temporal and not atemporal. Second, he suggests that we should view the relationship between time and eternity as akin to a three-dimensional being's relationship to two-dimensional space. Our relationship with our spatio-temporal environment is structured in accordance with the fact that we can navigate three dimensions of space. A two-dimensional creature would be more limited than us in this respect, and would likely have as much trouble imagining moving in three spatial dimensions as we would have in imagining having sudden access to a fourth spatial dimension. Wilkinson draws an analogy between this and God's relationship to time. Eternity, on this view, is similar to an additional temporal dimension that we are currently unable even to conceptualise let alone access.

In applying this to the context of the new creation, Wilkinson asserts several things. He claims that time must be present in new creation, as it is essential to both narratives of meaning and the development of relationships (core components of any new creation). He also argues that change will be a part of the new creation, but only positive changes like the restoration and renewal that accompanies resurrection, thus time is decoupled from decay. Moreover, though we will experience time in the new creation, it will not be a limiting factor as it is in the old creation. To emphasise this, Wilkinson echoes the New Testament writers' depictions of the risen Jesus who seems to be a temporal being without being constrained by time as ordinary persons are.

Most importantly, Wilkinson employs the concept of prolepsis – the idea that the eschatological future is already present in creation following the death and resurrection of Jesus. We are living in 'in-between times'; in our midst the new creation is already partially being made manifest. In this way, continuity is ensured between this reality and the next. New creation is, on this view, already ontologically present in the higher dimensions of time to which humanity does not yet have access. As Wilkinson writes, 'if new creation is the expanding the dimensions of this creation, then we are no longer limited by decay and we experience eternal life in all its "fullness"' (Wilkinson 2010: 133). Though Wilkinson himself points out the various physical problems with sustaining life on a multidimensional view of time, he argues that the new creation would not be subject to these.

Wilkinson also notes, with regard to matter, that modern physics teaches of the significance of treating complex systems *as systems* that are not reducible to their component parts. Quantum entanglement, chaos theory, and complexity theory, each stress that a holistic systems-level description is the only appropriate one in certain contexts. In exploring the continuity and discontinuity between our universe and the new creation, one must hold together the complex interrelationships between mass, energy, patternicity, and information. He suggests that this idea can be further developed in dialogue with feminist theologies that cite the importance both of one's physical body as an integral part of one's identity and the necessity of understanding one's place in the world within wider networks of interpersonal, social, and cultural relationships (Wilkinson 2010: chapter 7.4). It is by preserving these features of space, time, and relationality that the new creation retains continuity with the old.

The new creation also requires the transformation of matter such that it is continuous (i.e. is recognisably the same person or universe) whilst being discontinuous with regard to its relationship with God and its soteriological state. What might such a transformation be like? One might look to the Eucharist, believed by the Christian to involve the transformation of matter from profane to sacred; from mere bread and wine to the body and blood of Christ himself. Whether this happens in reality or in perception alone, it can be cited as an example of God's ability to transform matter into something that participates in the eschatological future.

As I have already argued, what is of utmost importance here is the context of relationships in which the transformed matter is located. Nothing eschatologically significant exists in isolation – eschatology is ultimately about networks of relationships, contextual as well as personal renewal, and thus the transformation *together* of everything created. Following Polkinghorne's idea that the soul, an information-bearing pattern, could be resurrected onto a new body (like old software on new hardware), one might understand the new creation to be a preservation of the information-bearing patterns of the context and relationality of this creation onto new 'hardware' of a transformed creation. Of course, important relational aspects (primarily of the relationships between creatures and creator) will be transformed, but the relational networks of the old creation would be able to persist despite the annihilation of old space, time, matter, and energy.

Keith Ward has suggested that the transformation of material into entirely new, eschatologically redeemed, forms is a plausible means by which God could manifest the new creation out of the old. Such a transformation could generate entirely new properties out of old matter-energy, perhaps in ways that would overcome the fundamental limitations of the old creation. He writes: 'no one could have foreseen that quarks and leptons could generate consciousness, and no one knows how it happened. But it did. So it may be that further transformations of the material will generate higher forms of consciousness, which would not be subject to physical decay' (Ward 2002: 246). Though we are unable to imagine what this higher form of consciousness would be like, this does not rule it out in principle. Nevertheless, Ward acknowledges that this speculative proposal may not be a state in which the resurrected dead could share, at least in the same bodies that they lived in. Therefore, whilst it could be seen as a natural extension of the Christian faith, it cannot be the whole story.

Polkinghorne suggests that the new creation will be *creatio ex vetere* – creating the new out of materials provided by the old. More specifically, this refers to God transforming the universe (that was originally created *ex nihilo* – out of nothing) beginning with the resurrection of Jesus. The new creation will be a totally sacramental world, free of suffering, suffused with the divine presence. Polkinghorne also argues that the new creation will be panentheist, such that all of creation will be God whilst God exists apart from creation also. On this view, the old creation of spacetime and matter will be transformed into a new creation that enjoys intimate relationality with the divine. Individuals would be resurrected in accordance with the information-centric view of personhood and the soul as being constituted primarily by information-bearing-patternicity discussed in (Section 4.2.1). Continuity and discontinuity are preserved to varying extents, depending on what constituted the 'stuff' out of which the new creation is formed. If the 'stuff' is physical matter, energy, etc., then the view emphasises continuity; if the 'stuff' out of which new creation is made is information that requires entirely new hardware, then this view accentuates discontinuity. Either way, the new creation will be entirely new with regard to its soteriological state and relationship with God.

One is able to overcome the threats posed by *freeze* or *fry* scenarios on the first reading, as the destruction of the physical universe would not entail destruction of the information-bearing patterns remembered in the mind of God. However, this reading of Polkinghorne comes at the high price of stark discontinuity concerning the physical substance of the old creation. God *could* create new matter to bear the old information, but in so doing he would sever the interconnectedness of information and matter that underlies this creation. It is a distinctly dualist proposal that relegates matter to lower, indeed disposable, ontological status. Whether this is acceptable is an open question. If one reads Polkinghorne with an emphasis on the *ex vetere* aspect of his view, this transformation will need to take place before *freeze* or *fry* become reality.

Using insights from contemporary cosmology, Russell, too, addresses what he calls this 'profound' challenge to Christian eschatology (Russell 2002b: 272). He distinguishes between what a scientific theory predicts (e.g. *freeze* or *fry*) and the philosophical assumption that this will necessarily come to pass.

It is quite possible, he writes, to expect that our current understanding of the physics at hand is either incorrect or that the laws on which it is based may change over the extraordinarily lengthy time scales with which this physics is concerned. Moreover, an omnipotent creator God is free to act in radically new ways that cannot be predicted by the laws of nature. Indeed, the theist should actively *expect* God to do so when transforming the universe into a new creation. *Freeze* or *fry* might have been inevitable had God not acted at Easter to raise Jesus from the dead and bring the promise of a new eschatological future into the finite realm of creaturely existence. As God did act, however, these predictions can no longer be accepted with certainty.

Taking this line of argument could be accused of illegitimately disengaging from the problem by denying that *freeze* or *fry* will occur. The entire enterprise of science and religion depends upon trust that the scientific disciplines provide valuable, accurate, insights into the functioning of the natural world that can inform theological reflection. By pursuing this route, Russell risks cherry-picking the parts of science that conform to his worldview and eschewing or denying those that do not. Nevertheless, it is consistent with theism that God may act with radical freedom to suspend or violate laws of nature. Indeed, the doctrine of eschatology seemingly requires God to do so. Given this, the problem for Russell may not be as severe as it first appeared.

Russell places the emphasis on discontinuity, endorsing Polkinghorne's *creatio ex vetere* and the significance of total eschatological transformation. Russell suggests that this may well include 'the radical transformation of the background conditions of space, time, matter, and causality, and with this, a permanent change in at least most of the present laws of nature' (Russell 2002b: 296). Nevertheless, attributes of this creation that are essential to human existence, the ability to form relationships (with persons human and divine), and other theologically valuable components will persist. For example, we can expect time to feature in new creation, as it is integral to human experience. Yet we can also expect the new temporality to be untainted by the loss of the past and the frustrating not-yet-ness of the future.

Despite this emphasis on discontinuity, Russell argues that one must also accept a certain level of 'realised eschatology', namely that the new creation is in some sense already manifesting in present creation. This secures continuity between this creation and the new creation, which stems from prolepsis. Following this, Russell suggests that the future can manifest concretely in the present, helping to imbue the present with spiritual significance. Moreover, his proposed understanding of prolepsis 'includes a strikingly new topological view of the relation between creation and the New Creation. Such a topology would allow the eschatological future to "reach back" and be revealed in the event of the resurrection of Jesus' (Russell 2012: 320). This topology, which connects present creation to the new creation *here and now*, is only describable theologically. He develops this argument in dialogue with Wolfhart Pannenberg's work in *Time in Eternity: Pannenberg, Physics, and Eschatology in Creative Mutual Interaction* (Russell 2012).

Wilkinson argues that the physical matter of this creation must be present in the new creation, even if it obeys different physical laws or is rearranged differently. He also emphasises how essential context and relationality will be in striking the right balance of continuity and discontinuity between this creation and the next. At the core of Wilkinson's response to the threat to eschatology from modern cosmology lies the resurrection of Jesus, which serves as the model for eschatological hope. Woven throughout this image is the necessity of death in the eschatological process – one cannot rise again if one does not die. Therefore, we should not be too concerned with the distant annihilation of the universe, any more than we should be concerned about the inevitability of our own death. Christianity teaches that the universe will be transformed; as this universe comes to an end, an eschatological new dawn will break. Death and destruction are as integral to this process as the resurrection itself. Ward echoes this, writing that 'the Christian faith is wholly consistent with the idea that this space-time will have a temporal end. Christians do not hope for a continuation of this space-time, just as it is, forever' (Ward 2002: 246). Thus, the Christian should not be too concerned about *freeze* or *fry* scenarios. They may, according to Ward and Wilkinson, trust in the hope of a new creation in the future.

Whilst the previous discussion does make substantial steps toward addressing the problem at hand, I argue that it addresses only one part of the conjunction that sits at its heart. That is, the conjunction of *presentism* and *freeze* or *fry* scenarios. The Christian reader may find the various responses to *freeze* or *fry* scenarios promising, grounded as they all are in the resurrection of Jesus Christ. Yet a sufficient rebuttal of the entire problem requires one to address the issue raised by this in an explicitly presentist context: the universe's end entails the complete disappearance into the unreal past of everything that has ever existed, human beings and physical creation alike. Meaning *nothing is left to be resurrected*. Whilst this solves the problem posed in Section 4.1 by entailing the annihilation of past sin, it carries the unfortunate consequence of annihilating the sinner along with it. Even if God acts before *freeze* or *fry* takes place, the bodies of most human beings will have decayed and disappeared into the non-existence of the past.

Despite the illuminating work of Russell, Polkinghorne, Ward, and Wilkinson, it remains the case that the inevitable end of the spatio-temporal universe raises significant problems for Christian eschatology that have not been wholly addressed. Therefore, I will end with the suggestion that if the Christian wishes to retain the continuity between old and new creation that is essential to the biblical witness, then *freeze* or *fry* end-time scenarios encourage her to reject presentism. The best route forward is to endorse either a four-dimensional block universe model of spacetime or the growing-block variant of the A-theory (which, incidentally, will no longer bear any material differences with the block universe once the final event in the universe has transpired). Only then can matter and spacetime continue to exist when the final events of the universe have unfolded, leaving them available to fulfil God's eschatological purposes.

5 Final Remarks

The aim of this Element has been to explore problems for both God and salvation that arise from the nature of spacetime. In order to achieve this, I first laid the intellectual foundations, tracking the development of philosophical and theological reflections on time in the Ancient and Medieval periods. These discussions are, in many ways, echoed in modern scholarship on the relationship between 'God and time' and 'spacetime and soteriology'. Understanding these seminal works is, therefore, highly useful when approaching the current field. I also summarised some leading time-focused debates happening in contemporary analytic philosophy, as these provide the conceptual and linguistic architecture within which the theological problems under consideration can be expressed. I then examined leading scientific approaches to understanding the nature of time and space, arguing that these are more consonant with a block universe (although A-theoretic, specifically presentist, interpretations do attract some support). With the physical and metaphysical groundwork laid, I turned to debates on God and time, a question that has been widely written on, and continues to be a lively area of scholarship.

After elucidating these important but preliminary considerations, I was able to proceed with the Element's primary purpose: exploring the implications of the two leading interpretations of spacetime for the doctrines of salvation and eschatology. If one is a B-theorist or C-theorist, subscribing to a four-dimensional block universe spacetime ontology, then one faces the problem of soteriological change in a static universe. Insofar as salvation requires a change in time, the static nature of the block universe and its prohibition of ontological change proves troublesome. I argued that one can begin to overcome this problem by endorsing a subjective understanding of personal salvation. If one endorses the alternative 3+1 spacetime ontology, combined with presentism (a highly popular position among theists), then one faces the problem of *freeze* or *fry*. Contemporary cosmology predicts that universe will end, and its contents will vanish into the obscurity of an unreal past. On this view, any eschatological commitment to bodily resurrection and the transformation of the physical stuff of this creation into a new creation is highly problematised. There are some promising solutions available, but I argue that they have not adequately addressed the specific problem a presentist spacetime ontology raises.

I end with the hope that the preceding pages have indicated how informative true interdisciplinarity can be. Academia is becoming increasingly specialised, and with it often comes the fragmentation of disciplines that used to be pursued in tandem (for example via natural philosophy). Though this increasing specialisation often brings highly valuable insights, too much compartmentalisation can lead to a certain amount of intellectual tunnel vision. The discipline of 'science and religion' is a highly effective antidote to this trend, and its successes disclose interdisciplinarity's rich potential. The nature of spacetime has proved a wealthy resource for engaging the doctrines of salvation and eschatology. I hope others will take up where this volume leaves off – there is plenty more to be discovered.

References

Anderson, E. (2012). 'Problem of Time in Quantum Gravity'. *Annalen der Physik*, 524(12), pp. 757–86.

St. Augustine. (2005). *Confessions*. Book XI (E. B. Pusey, trans.). Reprinted in Hoy and Oaklander.

Balashov, Y., & Janssen, M. (2003). 'Review: Presentism and Relativity'. *The British Society for the Philosophy of Science*, 54, pp. 327–46.

Barbour, J. (1999). *The End of Time*. New York: Oxford University Press.

Bardon, A. (2013). *A Brief History of the Philosophy of Time*. New York: Oxford University Press.

Baron, S., & Miller, K. (2019). *An Introduction to the Philosophy of Time*. Cambridge: Polity Press.

Barth, K. (1933). *The Epistle to the Romans*. Oxford: Oxford University Press.

Bobier, C. A. (2021). 'Revisiting Anselm on Time and Divine Eternity'. *Heythrop Journal*, 62(4), pp. 665–79.

Bohm, D. (2006). *The Special Theory of Relativity*. London: Routledge Classics.

Broad, C. D. (1923). *Scientific Thought*. London: Kegan Paul.

Broad, C. D. (1938). *An Examination of McTaggart's Philosophy*. Cambridge: Cambridge University Press.

Brook, A. (2013). 'Kant and Time-Order Idealism'. In A. Bardon & H. Dyke (eds.), *A Companion to the Philosophy of Time*. 1st ed. Somerset: Blackwell 120–135.

Cameron, R. P. (2015). *The Moving Spotlight: An Essay on Time and Ontology*. Oxford: Oxford University Press.

Craig, W. L. (1985). 'Was Thomas Aquinas a B- Theorist of Time?' *The New Scholasticism*, 59(4), pp. 475–83.

Craig, W. L. (1999). 'The Eternal Present and Stump-Kretzmann Eternity'. *American Catholic Philosophical Quarterly*, 73(4), pp. 521–36.

Craig, W. L. (2000). *The Tensed Theory of Time: A Critical Examination*. Dordrecht: Kluwer Academic.

Craig, W. L. (2001). *God, Time and Eternity*. Dordrecht: Kluwer Academic.

Dainton, B. (2011). 'Time, Passage, and Immediate Experience'. In C. Callender (ed.), *The Oxford Handbook of Philosophy of Time* (pp. 382–419). Oxford: Oxford University Press.

Deng, N. (2013). 'On Explaining Why Time Seems to Pass'. *The Southern Journal of Philosophy*, 51, pp. 367–82.

Deng, N. (2019a). *God and Time*. Cambridge: Cambridge University Press.

Deng, N. (2019b). 'One Thing after Another: Why the Passage of Time is Not an Illusion'. In A. Bardon, V. Arstila, S. Power, & A. Vatakis (eds.), *The Illusions of Time: Philosophical and Psychological Essays on Timing and Time Perception* (pp. 3–15). Basingstoke: Palgrave Macmillan.

Dyke, H. (2021). *Time*. Elements in Metaphysics. Cambridge: Cambridge University Press.

Einstein, A. (2010 [1920]). *Relativity: The Special and General Theory* (R. W. Lawson, trans.). Mansfield Centere: Martino.

Farr, M. (2020). 'C-Theories of Time: On the Adirectionality of Time'. *Philosophy Compass*, 15(12), pp. 1–17.

Farr, M. (forthcoming). 'Perceiving Direction in Directionless Time'. In K. M. Jaszczolt (ed.), *Understanding Human Time*. Oxford University Press.

Fiddes, P. (1989). *Past Event and Present Salvation: The Christian Idea of Atonement*. London: Darton, Longman & Todd.

Gallagher, S. (2013). 'Husserl and the Phenomenology of Temporality'. In A. Bardon & H. Dyke (eds.), *A Companion to the Philosophy of Time* (pp. 135-150) . 1st ed. Somerset: Blackwell.

Goris, H. (2003). 'Interpreting Eternity in Thomas Aquinas'. In G. Jaritz & G. Moreno-Riaño (eds.), *Time and Eternity: The Medieval Discourse*. Turnhout: Brepols. Electronic Resource.

Grünbaum, A. (1967). 'The Status of Temporal Becoming'. *Annals of the New York Academy of Sciences*, 138, pp. 374–95.

Grünbaum, A. (1971). 'The Meaning of Time'. In E. Freeman & W. Sellars (eds.), *Basic Issues in the Philosophy of Time* (pp. 195–228). La Salle, Illinois: Open Court.

Helm, P. (2014). 'Thinking Eternally'. In W. E. Mann (ed.), *Augustine's Confessions: Philosophy in Autobiography* (pp. 135–154). Oxford: Oxford Scholarship Online.

Holland, R. A. (2012). *God, Time and Incarnation*. Oregon: Wipf and Stock.

Hoy, R. C. (2013). 'Heraclitus and Parmenides'. In A. Bardon & H. Dyke (eds.), *A Companion to the Philosophy of Time* (pp. 9-29). 1st ed. Somerset: Blackwell.

Ives, H. E., & Stilwell, G. R. (1938). 'An Experimental Study of the Rate of a Moving Atomic Clock'. *Journal of the Optical Society of America*, 28(7), pp. 215–216.

Kennedy, R. J., & Thorndike, E. M. (1932). 'Experimental Establishment of the Relativity of Time'. *Physical Review*, 42(3), pp. 400–18.

Latham, A., Miller, K., & Norton, J. (2019). 'Is Our Naïve Theory of Time Dynamical?' *Synthese*. Vol. 198 (5), pp. 4251–4271 .

Latham, A., Miller, K., & Norton, J. (2020). 'An Empirical Investigation of Purported Passage Phenomenology'. *Journal of Philosophy*, 117, pp. 353–86.

Le Poidevin, R. (2007). *The Images of Time: An Essay on Temporal Representation*. Oxford: Oxford University Press.

Le Poidevin, R. (2016). '"Once For All": The Tense of the Atonement'. *European Journal for Philosophy of Religion*, 8(4), pp. 179–94.

Leftow, B. (1990). 'Aquinas on Time and Eternity'. *American Catholic Philosophical Quarterly*, 64(3), pp. 387–99.

Leftow, B. (1991). *Time and Eternity*. Ithaca: Cornell University Press.

Leftow, B. (2005). 'Eternity and Immutability'. In W. Mann (ed.), *The Blackwell Guide to the Philosophy of Religion* (pp.48–77). Oxford: Blackwell.

Leftow, B. (2009). 'Anselmian Presentism'. *Faith and Philosophy*, 26, pp. 297–319.

Lewis, D. (1984). 'Eternity Again: A Reply to Stump and Kretzmann'. *International Journal for Philosophy of Religion*, 15(1/2), pp. 73-79.

Mann, W. E. (2014). *Augustine's Confessions: Philosophy in Autobiography*. Oxford: Oxford Scholarship Online.

Marenbon, J. (2003). *Boethius*. Oxford: Oxford University Press.

Maudlin, T. (2012). *Philosophy of Physics: Space and Time*. Princeton: Princeton University Press.

Maudlin, T. (2019). *Philosophy of Physics: Quantum Theory*. Princeton: Princeton University Press.

McFarland, I. (2007). 'The Fall and Sin'. In J. Webster, K. Tanner, & I. R. Torrance (eds.), *The Oxford Handbook of Systematic Theology* (pp. 140–59). Oxford: Oxford University Press.

McGinnis, J. (2013). 'Creation and Eternity in Medieval Philosophy'. In A. Bardon & H. Dyke (eds.), *A Companion to the Philosophy of Time* (pp.73–87). 1st ed. Somerset: Blackwell.

McGrath, A. (2019). *The Territories of Human Reason: Science and Theology in an Age of Multiple Rationalities*. Oxford: Oxford University Press.

McTaggart, J.M.E. (1908). 'The Unreality of Time', *Mind*, 17(68), pp. 457–474.

Moltmann, J. (1974). *The Crucified God* (R. A. Wilson & J. Bowden, trans.). London: SCM Press.

Moltmann, J. (2002). 'Cosmos and Theosis: Eschatological Perspectives on the Future of the Universe'. In G. F. R. Ellis (ed.), *The Far-Future Universe: Eschatology from a Cosmic Perspective* (pp. 249–266). Philadelphia: Templeton Foundation Press.

Mozersky, J. (2011). 'Presentism'. In C. Callender (ed.), *The Oxford Handbook of Philosophy of Time* (pp. 122–144). Oxford: Oxford University Press.

Mullins, R T. "Doing Hard Time: Is God the Prisoner of the Oldest Dimension?" The Journal of Analytic Theology 2 (2014): 160–85.

Mullins, R. T. (2016). 'The End of the Timeless God'. *Oxford Studies in Analytic Theology*. Oxford: Oxford University Press.

Newton, I. (1686). *Philosophiae Naturalis Principia Mathematica*. London: Joseph Streater. Reproduced in facsimile by William Dawson & Sons.

Padgett, A. (1992). *God, Eternity and the Nature of Time*. New York: St. Martin's.

Page, B. (2018). 'If Anyone is in Christ – New Creation!' *Religious Studies*, Vol.56 (4), pp. 1–17.

Paul, L. (2010). 'Temporal Experience'. *Journal of Philosophy*, 107, pp. 333–59.

Peacocke, A. (2000). 'Science and the Future of Theology: Critical Issues'. *Zygon*, 35(1), pp. 119–40.

Phillips, I. (2009). 'The Images of Time: An Essay on Temporal Representation by Robin Le Poidevin' (review). *British Journal for the Philosophy of Science*, 60, pp. 439–46.

Polkinghorne, J. (1994). *Science and Christian Belief*. London: SPCK.

Polkinghorne, J. (2002). *The God of Hope and the End of the World*. New Haven: Yale University Press.

Prosser, S. (2013). 'The Passage of Time'. In A. Bardon & H. Dyke (eds.), *A Companion to the Philosophy of Time* (pp. 315–27). Somerset: John Wiley.

Putnam, H. (1967). 'Time and Physical Geometry'. *Journal of Philosophy*, 64, pp. 240–7.

Qureshi-Hurst, E. (2022). 'Anxiety, Alienation, and Estrangement in the Context of Social Media'. *Religious Studies*, 58(3) pp. 1–12.

Qureshi-Hurst, E. (2022). 'Can Sinners Really Change? Understanding Personal Salvation in the Block Universe'. *Zygon*, 57(2).

Qureshi-Hurst, E., & Pearson, A. (2020). 'Quantum Mechanics, Time, and Theology: Indefinite Causal Order and a New Approach to Salvation'. *Zygon*, 55(3), pp. 663–84.

Rea, M. C., & Murray, M. J. (2008). *An Introduction to the Philosophy of Religion*. Cambridge: Cambridge University Press.

Read, J., & Qureshi-Hurst, E. (2021). 'Getting Tense about Relativity'. *Synthese*, 198, pp. 8103–25.

Rogers, K. (2007). 'Anselmian Eternalism: The Presence of a Timeless God'. *Faith and Philosophy*, 24, pp. 3–27.

Rovelli, C. (2009). 'Forget Time'. *Essay for FQXi Contest on the Nature of Time*, arxiv: 0903.3832v3.

Russell, B. (1996). *History of Western Philosophy*. Abingdon: Routledge.

Russell, R. J. (2002a). 'Bodily Resurrection, Eschatology and Scientific Cosmology'. In T. Peters, R. J. Russell, & M. Welker (eds.), *Resurrection: Theological and Scientific Assessments* (pp. 3–30). Grand Rapids: Eerdmans.

Russell, R. J. (2002b). 'Eschatology and Physical Cosmology: A Preliminary Reflection'. In G. F. R. Ellis (ed.), *The Far Future Universe: Eschatology from a Cosmic Perspective* (pp. 266–315). Radnor: Templeton Foundation Press.

Russell, R. J. (2012). *Time in Eternity: Pannenberg, Physics and Eschatology in Creative Mutual Interaction*. Notre Dame: Notre Dame University Press.

Russell, R. J. (2022). 'A Flowing Time Interpretation of Special Relativity via an Inhomogeneous Tense-as-Relational Ontology: A Comment on Saulson'. *Zygon*, 56 (4), pp. 943–5.

Sartre, J.-P., & Barnes, H. E. (1957). *Being and Nothingness: An Essay on Phenomenological Ontology*. London: Methuen.

Shapiro, L. A. (2012). 'Embodied Cognition'. In E. Margolis, R. Samuels, & S. P. Stich (eds.), *The Oxford Handbook of Philosophy of Cognitive Science* (pp. 119–46). Oxford: Oxford University Press.

Strobach, N. (2013). 'Zeno's Paradoxes'. In A. Bardon & H. Dyke (eds.), *A Companion to the Philosophy of Time* (pp. 30–47). 1st ed. Somerset: Blackwell.

Stump, E. (2003). *Aquinas*. London: Routledge.

Stump, E., & Kretzmann, N. (1981). 'Eternity'. *The Journal of Philosophy*, 78 (8), pp 429–458.

Stump, E., & Kretzmann, N. (1992). 'Eternity, Awareness, and Action'. *Faith and Philosophy*, 9(4), pp. 463–82.

Swinburne, R. (1993). 'God and Time'. In *Reasoned Faith* (pp. 204–222). Ithaca: Cornell University Press.

Swinburne, R. (2008). 'Cosmic Simultaneity'. In W. L. Craig & Q. Smith (eds.), *Einstein, Relativity and Absolute Simultaneity* (pp. 224–261). Oxford: Routledge.

Thiselton, A. C. (2000). *The First Epistle to the Corinthians*. Grand Rapids: Eerdmans.

Tillich, P. (1947). 'The Problem of Theological Method'. *The Journal of Religion*, 27, pp. 16–26.

Tillich, P. (1951). *Systematic Theology Vol.1*. Digswell Place: James Nisbet.

van Fraassen, B. C. (1985). *An Introduction to the Philosophy of Time and Space*. New York: Columbia University Press.

Wallace, R. (2022). 'The Wholeness of Humanity: Coleridge, Cognition, and Holistic Perception'. *Zygon*, 57(2), pp. 656–674.

Ward, K. (2002). 'Cosmology and Religious Ideas about the End of the World'. In G. F. R. Ellis (ed.), *The Far-Future Universe: Eschatology from a Cosmic Perspective* (pp. 235–248). Philadelphia: Templeton Foundation Press.

Wilkinson, D. (2010). *Christian Eschatology and the Physical Universe*. London : T & T Clark.

Wolterstorff, N., & Cuneo, T. (2010). *Inquiring about God*. Cambridge: Cambridge University Press.

Cambridge Elements ≡

The Problems of God

Michael L. Peterson
Asbury Theological Seminary

Michael Peterson is Professor of Philosophy at Asbury Theological Seminary. He is the author of *God and Evil* (Routledge); *Monotheism, Suffering, and Evil* (Cambridge University Press); *With All Your Mind* (University of Notre Dame Press); *C. S. Lewis and the Christian Worldview* (Oxford University Press); *Evil and the Christian God* (Baker Book House); and *Philosophy of Education: Issues and Options* (Intervarsity Press). He is co-author of *Reason and Religious Belief* (Oxford University Press); *Science, Evolution, and Religion: A Debate about Atheism and Theism* (Oxford University Press); and *Biology, Religion, and Philosophy* (Cambridge University Press). He is editor of *The Problem of Evil: Selected Readings* (University of Notre Dame Press). He is co-editor of *Philosophy of Religion: Selected Readings* (Oxford University Press) and *Contemporary Debates in Philosophy of Religion* (Wiley-Blackwell). He served as General Editor of the Blackwell monograph series Exploring Philosophy of Religion and is founding Managing Editor of the journal *Faith and Philosophy*.

About the Series

This series explores problems related to God, such as the human quest for God or gods, contemplation of God, and critique and rejection of God. Concise, authoritative volumes in this series will reflect the methods of a variety of disciplines, including philosophy of religion, theology, religious studies, and sociology

Cambridge Elements ☰

The Problems of God

Elements in the Series

Printed in the United States
by Baker & Taylor Publisher Services